The Root That Never Died

A Christian Woman's Journey
Back to Her Hebraic Heritage

Lisa Burkhardt Worley

The Root That Never Died
A Christian Woman's Journey
Back to Her Hebraic Heritage
By Lisa Burkhardt Worley

www.PearlsOfPromiseMinistries.com
Published by:
Pearls of Promise Ministries

To my dear friend Amy,
my Jewish sister forever

Table of Contents

Introduction

One of my favorite stories from the Tanakh centers around the Levitical priests (*kohanim*) carrying the Ark of the Covenant across the Jordan River. Hiking across the Jordan without drowning seemed as impossible to the Israelites as crossing the Red Sea had forty years earlier. However, the day before, their leader Joshua had prepped the Israelites for another Red Sea-like miracle, saying, "Consecrate yourselves, for tomorrow *ADONAI* will do wonders in your midst" (Joshua 3:5). And He did. The priests not only carried the Ark of the Covenant safely across the Jordan; they did it when the Jordan River was at *flood* stage.

However, safe passage was not without a catch. The priests were asked to take a stand of faith and trust *ADONAI* by stepping into the Jordan first, *prior* to the miracle. One source says the river at flood stage was probably a hundred feet wide and at least ten feet deep.[i] You don't need a rocket scientist to tell you that carrying an ark loaded with heavy stone tablets would normally issue a one-way ticket to the

1

river bottom. But G-d. As soon as the priests planted their feet in the swollen Jordan, *ADONAI* showcased His power. The water rose up in one heap a great distance away. The priests stood firmly on dry ground in the middle of the river, and the entire nation of Israel crossed over to the other side.

Have you ever watched G-d part the waters for you?

The call back to my Hebraic roots feels a little like stepping into the Jordan at flood stage. Through faith, I've jumped in with both feet. Everything is new, and I am leaning on *ADONAI* to guide me through this revamped way of looking at Christianity. Learning about the traditions and the festivals and, more importantly, seeing the Christian Bible from a Jewish perspective has required an unwavering trust in *ADONAI*. It's a call that has led to a move out of our longtime denomination and to an intentional study of the Bible through a "Jewish" lens, and it has also resulted in a "joint venture" with G-d as I enter a doctoral program with a Messianic Studies concentration.

But as I dive deeper into this flood of fresh waters, the more I am seeing and understanding the big picture that started with the Torah and ends with the book of Revelation. Because of His great love for His children, *ADONAI* developed a plan from the beginning so we could one day live in His presence, just like the old days when He and Adam and Eve broke bread together and admired the same lush scenery in Eden.

But YHWH is holy, and this restoration could not happen without a sacrifice—the sacrifice of an unblemished lamb, Yeshua HaMashiach, to atone for our sins. Yeshua, prophesied throughout Old-Testament Scripture, provided a gift beyond human capacity to give, and I am eternally grateful. Because of Yeshua's selfless sacrifice, the prospect of being in the same room as *ADONAI* one day is something I eagerly anticipate as we all draw closer to the appointed time.

This book recounts the journey back to my Hebraic roots, but it also shares the accounts of others who have discovered the scarlet and very "Jewish" thread that runs throughout the Word of G-d. In *The Root That Never Died,* I will also unveil what I've discovered about prophecy concerning the promised Messiah, Yeshua, as well as documented sightings of Yeshua in the Torah, the Prophets, and the Writings. Toward the end there will be a synopsis of the "end of days" yet to come, which are more obviously imminent every day.

I want to thank my faithful friend Frank Ball for formatting this book and Nonie Jobe for her superb editing work. I also want to say "toda" to my dear friend and gifted artist Debbie Jackson for providing the front and back cover art and the olive tree pictures inside. As you will soon discover, it perfectly represents *The Root That Never Died.*

Chapter 1
The Root

"You're my little Jew baby."

I spent many childhood years growing up in my grandparents' olive-green-painted ranch home in San Antonio, Texas, and this is how my grandmother "Nonnie" lovingly referred to me at times. I believe *ADONAI* used Nonnie to frequently remind me, from the beginning of my life as a towheaded little girl with deep-set hazel eyes, that there was something special about the Jewish heritage I inherited from my father. It is a bloodline I did not fully appreciate until much later in life.

My father, whose mother was an "Adler," hailed from rich Jewish roots, growing up in Winnetka, a suburb of Chicago, Illinois. The name "Adler" means "eagle" in English. During the 1800s many Jews, including my great-great grandfather, migrated to the Midwest; and by the turn of the twentieth century, there were about 270,000 living in the Chicago metroplex.[ii]

My great-great-grandfather's name was Leopold Adler. He immigrated from Baden, Germany, to the Windy City, where he became a successful clothing merchant. Meanwhile, his wife Rose spent her days chasing toddlers around. She gave birth to seven children, including my great-grandmother, Harriet Adler. Harriet's brother Manasseh (Max) married into the Sears-Roebuck family, became a vice president at Sears, and was a well-known philanthropist who founded the Adler Planetarium in Chicago. Max came up with the idea after traveling to Germany, where he visited several planetariums, including the Deutsches Museum. Julius Rosenwald, Max's brother-in-law and the president of Sears, was also inspired by the Deutsches Museum and founded the Museum of Science and Industry in Chicago.[iii]

Meanwhile, Harriet gave birth to my grandmother, Helen, who became a stenographer and married Charles Burkhardt, a local furniture salesman. Their three offspring included my father, William Lincoln Burkhardt, and his two siblings, Alice and Charles, Jr.

While there is no denying the Jewish lineage of my family, my great-grandmother Harriet turned away from practicing Judaism and embraced Christian Science, something she passed down to my grandmother Helen as well. For many years, I held onto a miniature Bible that belonged to my grandmother. It was a treasured possession that, unfortunately, was lost in one of the many moves over my lifetime. Because I never had a relationship with my paternal grandmother, I do not know to this day where her Jewish faith ranked in her life.

My father, Dr. William Burkhardt, studied at Northwestern University in Chicago, where he earned his medical degree, but he settled in San Antonio, Texas, by way of a stint in the Air Force. Based at Randolph Air Force Base, he was a practicing Air Force doctor who also conducted research for the military by constructing and running tests on hyperbaric chambers. He and a colleague, Dr. Harry F. Adler (no relation), worked together and produced articles far above my pay grade—documented research like "The Effect of Various Drugs on Psychomotor Performance at Ground Level and at Stimulated Altitudes of 18,000 Feet in a Low-Pressure Chamber" and "Decompression Sickness: Some Factors Which Affect the Bends at Altitude."

I am grateful to Dr. Adler for sharing every memory he had of my dad. He told me my father was "an honest, outgoing, and energetic human being who could relate to anybody. He went first class." He also said Dr. Burkhardt often repeated a French saying, "Cela viendra," which means "It will come." It was Dr. Adler's feeling that in my father's mind it meant he would make it big one day.

And when my dad retired from the Air Force and established a medical practice in San Antonio, Texas, he did make it big for a while. My six-foot-one blonde and lean father was a popular and beloved local physician in an affluent suburb of San Antonio known as Alamo Heights. He played competitive polo every Sunday and participated in equestrian events for enjoyment. He was also a skeet shooter and a water skier during free time.

When my dad met my mother, he was already twice-divorced with a teenage daughter. Their brief journey together began on a blind date. My mother said my father picked her up in a Jaguar and was wearing a flashy sequin tie. Because of his unusual attire, she thought he was a "sissy." However, it turned into a whirlwind romance that culminated at the altar. The newlyweds bought a big house in Terrell Hills, a city adjoining Alamo Heights, and together the two enjoyed the "American dream."

I do not know where my father's Jewish heritage stood in his life either, but I know that he was very "Jewish" in appearance. He had deep-set eyes like mine, a rather large nose, and kinky-curly hair that he buzzed off in a crew cut. His blond hair may have thrown people off, but that was probably handed down from the Burkhardt side of the family tree. He also possessed what I would call "chutzpah," a Yiddish term that means "impudence or gall." Dr. Adler wrote this about their first week of serving in the Air Force:

> After two days I noticed that Bill and I never had to do guard duty, KP as dishwashers, police the grounds (which means picking up paper, cigarette butts, etc.) and nothing else except attend classes. All night long everybody else was being awakened for something. "Bill," says I. "How come we never have to do anything?" He began to laugh. Then on the day we left our training in Battle Creek, he told me. "I found

the Sergeant who made out the duty rosters and incidentally told him that in a few days you would be an officer and stationed in Battle Creek and that it wouldn't hurt to have you for a friend." It hurt nobody. It was chutzpah. It was Bill's way of adapting to a situation so that he could enjoy it.

Since my grandmother seemed so keenly aware of my "Jewishness," I have to believe that my father talked about his heritage and never forgot his Jewish roots as well. Otherwise, the subject wouldn't have come up, and I wouldn't have been such an oddity to her.

One day, before a small crowd that included my mother and my half-sister Lori, the American dream morphed into the American nightmare. It was a day that would affect the lives of many. My father, Dr. Bill Burkhardt, was competing in the heat of his usual Sunday afternoon polo match when he collapsed and fell off his pony. Emergency medical personnel were summoned, but it was too late. My pregnant and shell-shocked mother, Barbara, jumped into the ambulance to cling to what life was left in my father, but he didn't make it to the hospital. He died of a massive heart attack at age thirty-nine.

I was born two months later.

The Jewish period of mourning is called "Aninut." It is the stretch of time between learning of one's death and the burial. There are seven days of mourning after that called "shiva," and the entire mourning period is referred to as "sheloshim."

While the specified grieving period is not supposed to extend beyond the allotted time, I believe my mother's "sheloshim" never really ended. She suffered with mental illness the rest of her life as a direct result of the trauma she experienced at the Brackenridge Park Polo Grounds.

My half-sister, who claimed she was left alone that day, said she went through years of counseling to heal from what happened at the polo field. Years later, when she was living in Pennsylvania and I was residing three hours away in New York, I contacted her via phone and asked if we could visit and reconnect. Despite my coaxing, she refused. My half-sister died in 2012, and to this day I am still having a "sheloshim" of my own, mourning the loss of a sister-bond that never took root.

My Jewish father died before I was even born; and for all practical purposes, he alone had represented anything in my life that was Jewish. Any observance of Jewish holidays, like Rosh Hashanah, Passover, Yom Kippur, or any of the seven Levitical feasts, would never be a part of my journey—or so I thought. In a sense, all that remained of my Jewish family tree was a dead stump that used to be my father; and when I was born shortly after his death, I was only a little twig peeking out of what had once lived.

I'm told that from the moment I entered the world, I carried an eerie resemblance to my dad. I had the same blonde hair—wavy, but not as curly—deep-set eyes, and "the nose." The similarities may have been the reason my mother had trouble looking at me early on. The doctors who delivered me exclaimed, "She looks just like Bill!" So I was named "Lisa William" after my father.

Not long after I took my first breath, my Jewish grandmother and my father's sister, Aunt Alice, came to visit me. They saw my mother's depressed state and decided they wanted to bundle me up and take me back to Chicago, where they would raise me in my father's childhood stomping grounds. My maternal grandmother said, "You'll take this baby over my dead body!" After an unsuccessful attempt to relocate me to Chi-Town, Helen Wile and Alice Burkhardt returned home.

I experienced the consequence of that standoff eight years later when my paternal grandmother died. I received a letter containing her last will and testament, and in the documentation, it was clear that I had been disinherited; I received only $1.00 from my Jewish grandmother. The sting of that rejection is still there, but it was an early lesson that my inheritance is in heaven, and that my *ADONAI* Jireh (Provider) would take care of me during my time on earth. It would not be the first time I would be rejected by a Jewish family member, but for some reason that did not affect the way I looked at this special connection to G-d. There was always something mysterious and significant about the root; and as I continued through life, G-d kept it always before me.

Throughout the years, I believe G-d (in this case, *El Roi,* "*the G-d who sees*") picked up where my maternal grandmother "Nonnie" left off. He creatively used different means to remind me of my

"Jewishness." After living with my grandparents off and on until the middle of fourth grade, my mother moved back into the house she and my father bought when they were first married, and I grew up in a school district that probably had more Jewish kids enrolled than any other in the city. I remember being fascinated with some of the Jewish boys' intelligence—so brilliant—never thinking I was cut from the same tree.

That's because over the years I had been told repeatedly, "You're not Jewish," because it runs through the mother's bloodline; and since my mother was not Jewish, I am not Jewish. Just the other day, when I was speaking to a "Gentile" woman, I mentioned that I was Jewish as a result of having a Jewish father; and before I could complete my sentence, she exclaimed, "You're not Jewish. It has to go through the mother!" Today I wonder, how do you explain the DNA results I received from Ancestry.com, clearly showing that a high percentage of my genetic makeup includes Jewish blood, second only to my English roots? In addition, as I scan through my matches on Ancestry.com, there are Adler cousins but also cousins with the names "Pearlman," "Strauss," and "Rosenberg," all Jewish surnames.

I have done some research on this rule concerning the matrilineal viewpoint of Judaism, and it is my determination that this was not the way G-d initially designed His family tree. Shaye D. Cohen, the Littauer Professor of Hebrew Literature and Philosophy at Harvard University, has written a book and several articles on this issue. Cohen found that matrilineal descent evolved from an original policy of patrilineal descent. He said, "In the Torah, a person's status as a Jew seems to come from his father. Joseph was married to a non-Jewish woman, and his children were considered Jewish. The same was the case for Moses and King Solomon. The change to a policy of matrilineal descent came in late antiquity."[iv]

According to halachah (the totality of laws and ordinances that have evolved since biblical times to regulate religious observances and the daily life and conduct of the Jewish people), "Jewish status is determined on the basis of matrilineality; that is, the child of a Jewish mother is a Jew, even when the child's father is a Gentile. The offspring of a Gentile mother is a Gentile, even if the father is a Jew. Prior to the Rabbinic period (70-500 CE), we find little trace of the principal of matrilineal descent. The Bible in fact seems to recognize a purely patrilineal descent, regardless of the identity of the mother."[v] So the Reformed Jewish movement has moved away from this belief.

In 1983 the Central Conference of American Rabbis adopted the Resolution on Patrilineal Descent. According to this resolution, a child of one Jewish parent who is raised exclusively as a Jew and whose Jewish status is "established through appropriate and timely public and formal acts of identification with the Jewish faith and people" is Jewish. These "acts of identification" include entry into the covenant, acquisition of a Hebrew name, Torah study, bar/bat mitzvah, and confirmation.[vi]

I knew none of this as I proceeded in life. I just knew I had a Jewish father but thought I was not really Jewish. However, G-d continued to show me there was something slowly growing out of what I thought was a dead stump that would not be in full bloom until many years later.

Meanwhile, I chose an unusual career for women in the late seventies and early eighties—television sportscasting. When I was working in my first job, at the ABC affiliate in Chattanooga, Tennessee, I received two separate, unexpected calls from the rabbis who led congregations in the area. They both invited me to worship at their synagogues. I thought that was odd, since my last name was "Burkhardt," not the Jewish "Adler" name I descended from. I politely told them I was a Christian and that my father was Jewish. They both seemed disappointed and said I could be a "friend" of their synagogues, but I tucked this memory away. I believe it was a sign that there was something supernatural about the heritage within me, that even I could not see at the time, but others sensed. It was another reminder from G-d that I was a Jewish girl.

After three years in Chattanooga, my career moved me back to San Antonio, Texas, where I went to work for the CBS affiliate. That was a stretch of major change in my life. Shortly after I landed in my home town, I met my Gentile husband, Jeff. After six months of dating, I got engaged to this corn-fed Iowa native, and we married six months after that. Two years after we met, we bought our first house. Little did we know we would become close friends with another family who lived on the same cul-de-sac and happened to be Jewish.

The only problem (especially for my husband's bank account) was that the Sadovskys were jewelers; to this day I love pretty jewelry, so we gave them *a lot* of business. I remember one weekend when we had several neighbor families over for dinner. One of the neighbors had been checking out the Sadovsky's jewelry brought a stunning diamond bracelet over to the house. It had a rather large price tag, and she meant it as a joke when she said, "Jeff needs to buy you this." At that moment I fell in love with the 14k gold bracelet with diamonds encased by gold ovals; needless to say, after many payments, it was mine. Unfortunately, years later that beloved bracelet slipped off my wrist, never to be seen again. There is a Proverb I should have listened to: "Death and Destruction are never satisfied, and neither are human eyes" (Proverbs 27:20, NIV). Perhaps the bracelet should have remained in the box.

Knowing my Jewish heritage, the Sadovskys would often invite us to their family Seders, and we were also guests at their sons' Bar Mitzvahs. In turn, we would ask them over to help us decorate the Christmas tree, and they would be invited to join our Christmas dinners. I think we mutually enjoyed participating in each other's traditions. For me, though, it was an early introduction to celebrating Jewish holidays that I later instituted into my own yearly calendar.

I spent about five years in San Antonio before I received a big career break. I accepted an offer to

15

take a national reporting position with the HBO Sports program, *Inside the NFL*. As a part of my interview for that job, I was asked to interview Marty Glickman. Glickman, a New York institution, had been the voice of the Jets, the Giants, and the New York Knicks, but had also been a teammate on the 1936 Olympic track team when they competed in Berlin, Germany. Scheduled to run in the 4 x 100 relay, Glickman, who was Jewish, and his Jewish teammate Sam Stoller were replaced at the last minute by Jesse Owens and Ralph Metcalfe. Glickman believed that US Olympic Track Coaches Dean Cromwell and Avery Brundage were motivated by anti-Semitism and the desire to spare the Führer Adolph Hitler the embarrassing sight of two American Jews on the winning podium.[vii] It was an honor to interview Glickman. I was hired by HBO Executive Producer Ross Greenburg, also Jewish, and I believe it was another leg of my Jewish journey.

A year later, I received a second big-break opportunity. Jeff and I, along with our eight-month-old son Kyle, moved to the New York City area, where I became an anchor for the regional sports program *MSG Sportsdesk* on the Madison Square Garden Network. I also continued working for *Inside the NFL*.

As I look back at my Jewish journey, I find it interesting that we "happened" to settle in New Rochelle, a heavily Jewish-populated community. New Rochelle is located in Westchester County, about a thirty-minute train ride from New York City, and its population is about 17 percent Jewish. Several notable Jewish Americans were raised in New Rochelle, including *Fiddler on the Roof* composer Jerry Bock, Union of Reform Judaism president Rabbi Rick Jacobs, and *West Wing* actor Joshua Malina.[viii]

Because of the large Jewish contingent, there are several synagogues in New Rochelle. We lived down the street from an orthodox synagogue; and as we ran errands on Saturday (before my understanding of taking a Shabbat rest), I was always amazed at the congregants *walking* from their homes to their service on the Shabbat. I always thought it would be wonderful if Christians were as devout as these Jewish sisters and brothers.

Interestingly, one of my two closest friends in New Rochelle was married to a Jewish man, a successful Wall Street attorney. He had a musical gift, and I recall going back to their house many nights after a couples' dinner out and singing while he played the piano. I loved those get-togethers. There was a kinship there I didn't understand at the time; but as I reflected later, it must have been something to do with the tribal Jewish blood that ran through both of our veins.

When we left New York about three-and-a-half years later, we returned to our old house in San Antonio that we had rented out, into our same neighborhood with the Sadovskys. We seemed to pick up right where we left off, but I also added another Jewish sister, Amy.

When Amy and I were introduced at a lunch date with a mutual friend, we hit it off immediately. We both loved to shop, and we were both sports enthusiasts. (I also see shopping as a sport!) At the time, I was a racquetball player; but she got me into her sport, tennis, by convincing me it was more social, even though I never reached her level of play. When participating in league competition, I went all out and tore almost every muscle in my body. Aye yai yai! Amy and her husband Mark were our favorite dinner partners, and we would explore all the great restaurants in our mutual city. There was also an inexplicable bond with Amy that exists to this day. I found it interesting that she was from Pennsylvania, where my half-sister lived after my father died. It was as if *ADONAI* saw my despair and gave me a sister-friend for life to replace the sister I lost. Even though we have not lived in the San Antonio area for fifteen years, I still go back to visit; and when I do, I usually stay in Amy and Mark's guest house. It has been a friendship that has endured through the years.

However, I now believe my bond with Amy and the Sadovskys, our stay in New Rochelle, my work in New York (one of the most Jewish cities in the world), and the elementary school system I was planted in were all part of a much larger canvas that G-d was painting in my life; and as the entire work of art is being revealed, I see it is very "Jewish."

Chapter 2
The Shema

My television career lasted almost twenty years, but post television, I felt a call to seminary. Someone once said to me, "All Jewish people who find Yeshua end up in ministry." Well, it was at least true for me.

I was in the second semester of studies at Southern Methodist University's Perkins School of Theology when my Old Testament professor, Dr. Roy Heller, said, "If you see a biblical passage in both black and red letters, then you need to pay attention to it." The Torah mainstay we were looking at that day was one anyone who grew up in the Jewish faith would know and would have memorized. This passage is so important that it's often placed inside a Mezuzah (a case Jewish families attach to their doorposts containing a scroll with certain Scriptures written on it), so they're reminded of its significance as they enter their homes. At the time, I had no idea it was this exact commandment rolled up inside the Mezuzah. All I knew was that *ADONAI* was giving me a private lesson on the importance of this Scripture.

It's found in the Torah in Deuteronomy 6:4–9 and is referred to as the Shema. The word "Shema" in Hebrew means "hear," "obey," or "listen." In this case, G-d is saying, "Listen up; there is nothing more important!" According to Jewishlearning.com, "The Shema is the centerpiece of the daily morning and evening prayer services and is considered by some the most essential prayer in all of Judaism. An affirmation of G-d's singularity and kingship, its daily recitation is regarded by traditionally observant Jews as a biblical commandment."[ix]

However, this was my first encounter with the magnitude of the Shema, which reads: "Hear O Israel, the L-RD our G-d, the L-RD is one. Love *ADONAI* your G-d with all your heart and with all your soul and with all your strength. These words, which I am commanding you today, are to be on your heart. You are to teach them diligently to your children, and speak of them when you sit in your house, when you walk by the way, when you lie down and when you rise up. Bind them as a sign on your hand, they are to be as frontlets between your eyes, and write them on the doorposts of your house and on your gates."

Professor Heller then asked us to turn to Matthew 22:36–40, where Yeshua was asked by an expert in the law, "'Teacher, which is the greatest commandment in the Torah?' And He said to him, 'You shall love *ADONAI* your God with all your heart, and with all your soul, and with all your mind.'

This is the first and greatest commandment. And the second is like it, 'You shall love your neighbor as yourself.' The entire Torah and the Prophets hang on these two commandments.'" Hmmm . . . There it was in both black and red letters, and G-d was accentuating it's importance by starting my lesson with the "Shema."

The first verse of the Shema, from the sixth chapter of Deuteronomy, is among the best-known in all of Jewish liturgy. It is recited at the climactic moment of the final prayer of Yom Kippur, the holiest day of the year, and traditionally as the last words before death. It is also tradition to recite it with the hand placed over the eyes.

Dr. Greg Stone, who is Jewish and leads Jewish Ministries at Gateway Church in Southlake, Texas, says when Yeshua was asked to provide the greatest commandment and quoted the Shema, "There was no more 'Jewish' answer He could have given. That is the heart cry of Judaism." Yeshua was born Jewish, raised Jewish, and observed Jewish customs like the feasts. Dr. Stone continues, "His parents went to Jerusalem every year at the Feast of the Passover. And when He was twelve years old, they went up to Jerusalem according to the custom of the feast. He kept Sabbath. For example, two different Sabbaths are mentioned in Luke 6. And He did many miracles on the Sabbath. He honored the Sabbath."

So when Yeshua quoted the Shema as the most important commandment, I paid attention to the detail of the command to write the words on our doorframes and began to search for a "Love the

L-RD" plaque to place over my doorframe. I visited all the Christian gift shops in town. I searched online but could not find anything like it. That is when I decided to go into a local "mom and pop" gift store near our house. I asked the owner if she'd ever seen anything like what I was looking for. She said no, but she would check with a Louisiana-based artist, the founder of "Artstones by Heavenly Delights," who provided original plaques for their store.

As it turned out, the Bayou artist had never created this type of art piece, but she said she was looking for something new—so it was birthed. The artist designed the first ever "Love the L-RD your G-d" plaque that now sits over our door leading out to the garage. As I leave the house every day, it's a reminder that there is nothing more important for me to do than to love *ADONAI.* It's in black and red letters.

It's paramount to note that G-d may command us to love Him, but He was the one who invented love. He loved us first. 1 John 4:7–8 says, "Beloved, let us love one another, for love is from God, and whoever loves has been born of God and knows God. Anyone who does not love does not know God, because God is love."

King David of Israel was described by G-d as "a man after My own heart" (Acts 13:22, NIV), and I believe it was because of the overflowing love he had for his heavenly Father. You see this display of King David's heart through his obedience to G-d, but also in the Psalms he penned—especially Psalm 63, where David shared about his total reliance on G-d. He said, "O God, You are my God, earnestly I seek You. My soul thirsts for You. My flesh longs for You in a dry and weary land, where there is no water. So, I looked for You in the Sanctuary, to see Your power and Your glory. Since Your lovingkindness is better than life, my lips will praise You. So I will bless You as long as I live. In Your name I lift up my hands" (Psalm 63:2–5).

David loved G-d and G-d loved him, just as *ADONAI's* love pours out to us.

I first recognized the endless love of my heavenly Father through a devastating job loss. I was working in New York City at the top of my career in sportscasting, when in the same week both of my television contracts were not renewed. I plummeted from the top of the media mountain to the valley of anonymity, and this dramatic change in my livelihood required drastic measures. We could no longer afford our New Rochelle home and had to move farther north to Connecticut. Our hope was that if we lived closer to Bristol, Connecticut, where ESPN was located, I might latch onto that network and reboot my career.

And, like King David or another great patriarch Moses, I had my closest encounter with G-d during this time in the wilderness.

It was in the midst of great hardship and uncertainty that I suggested to my husband that we should connect with a church. I chose one randomly from the Yellow Pages, back when there was such a thing, and we visited a small Presbyterian congregation in Fairfield, Connecticut. Not long after we stepped inside the door, one of the matriarchs of the church put her arm around us and invited me to join a young mom's Bible study. "I think you will love the women doing this study, and it does offer childcare," the woman said. By that time, my son Kyle was about three years old. I felt wanted and accepted at this church, something I desperately needed after being rejected by my career, and I never visited another house of worship while living in Connecticut. More importantly, for the first time ever, I studied the Bible.

The study was based on the book of John in the New Testament. The gospel of John is considered the "love" gospel. John, who penned this book most likely in the latter part of the first century, was writing to the Christians in the province of Asia to provide a fuller understanding of the life and ministry of Jesus Christ.[x] John was one of two disciples of Yeshua who was not martyred, but he spent the latter years of his life in exile on the Island of Patmos, where he wrote the biblical book of Revelation.

The Bible is described as "living and active" and "sharper than any two-edged sword" and the words in the book of John began to pierce my heart. After studying through the "love" Gospel, I realized it was out of G-d's love that He reached out to me in the midst of my despair and brought His wayward daughter back into a relationship with Him. At some point, I was convicted of the sins I had committed over the desert years, and I surrendered every aspect of my life to my heavenly Father. From that juncture on, I began to love *ADONAI* "with all my heart,

24

with all my soul, and with all my strength." His desires became my desires. My goal was to serve Him, and when He did allow me to work for my dream employer, ESPN, I was grateful and saw this as a reward for my renewed heart.

One day, I was driving to Boston to meet a production crew to put together a story for ESPN on the NBA Celtics. It was about a three-hour commute from Stratford, Connecticut, where we now lived, to the Celtics training facility. At that time, I owned a Rod Stewart tape that featured the song, *Have I Told You Lately*. I began to see that song with spiritual eyes, and I sang it over and over at the top of my lungs to *ADONAI*. *Have I told you lately that I love you?* I was overflowing with love for my Redeemer, and I was letting Him know how much I loved Him through this song.

After that, I experienced a close encounter with G-d, one that I will never forget. Everywhere I went, the song *Have I Told You Lately* played—in the grocery store, in the drug store, and in the restaurant; and when I'd turn on the radio, there it was again. It was apparent that my loving Creator was showing me He heard my heart, and He was singing the song back to me.

Our G-d, the G-d of the Gentiles and the Jews, is merciful and loving. He wants us to spend time in His presence, and He wants us to know Him intimately. In Deuteronomy 7:9, the Torah reminds us, "Know therefore that *ADONAI* your God, He is God—the faithful God who keeps covenant kindness for a thousand generations with those who love Him and keep His *mitzvot*."

He has a special bond with His chosen ones, one that I would not personally discover until many years after I became an active student and follower of His, rather than a believer in word only. It's a connection like the one described in the book of Hosea, found in the prophetic writings of the Hebrew Bible. In this book, the L-RD tells the prophet Hosea to marry a promiscuous woman and have children with her. *ADONAI* was making a point. This marriage would be like His relationship with Israel—His chosen ones were also guilty of unfaithfulness. Yet Hosea took back the unfaithful wife, Gomer, and loved her, just as *ADONAI* continually welcomes His children when they repent and turn back to Him. After periods of discipline, administered as a way to draw us back, our Father's love flows again, both to Israel and to those who believe in Him and are obedient to His ways. Hosea 14:5 says, "I will heal their backsliding, I will love them freely, for My anger will turn away from him."

I've been recently reading about the kings of Israel and Judah. There was one common thread. If the king was faithful to *ADONAI*, kept all of His commandments, and taught his people to do the same, then his reign would have a longer life span. If he was labeled a bad king by doing evil in G-d's sight, the good times didn't last so long. But what I found is that with the L-RD it's never "Three strikes and you're out." If the king of Israel or Judah attempted to turn the country out of a moral tailspin and followed G-d's ways, then they received divine favor, which was birthed out of *ADONAI*'s love for His people. To this day, obedience is still the "main thing" when it comes to following our loving G-d.

In Ephesians 3, the apostle Paul prayed that we would be able to wrap our minds around the depth of *ADONAI*'s love for us. "I pray that from His glorious riches He would grant you to be strengthened in your inner being with power through His *Ruach*, so that Messiah may dwell in your hearts through faith. I pray that you, being rooted and grounded in love, may have strength to grasp with all the *kedoshim* what is the width and length and height and depth, and to know the love of Messiah which surpasses knowledge, so you may be filled up with all the fullness of God" (Ephesians 3:16–19).

As Paul said, it is a love that is beyond what our brains can comprehend, but He desires to fill us up to full capacity. It is out of His love that He pursued Israel, He pursued me when I plummeted into the deepest valley, and He pursues you, because He desires for you to enter a more intimate relationship with Him.

Chapter 3
The Land

By 2014, my television career had been long gone and I had worked in a public-relations job and attended seminary. I was now building my own ministry, Pearls of Promise, a ministry that helps my female sisters overcome brokenness and teaches women how to draw into a more intimate relationship with G-d. We added another son, Bret, to our fold seven years after we conceived Kyle. He was now in middle school, and our oldest had just graduated from Texas A & M University with a degree in computer engineering. To celebrate his accomplishment, we took a family trip to Barcelona, Spain, and Paris, France. We had a wonderful time exploring Europe together.

There's one memory from that trip I will never forget. It happened at the world-famous Louvre in Paris. We wanted to view the well-known Rembrandt painting, the *Mona Lisa,* but we were told there were too many people at the museum that day and we would not be able to negotiate the crowd to get into the room where it's displayed. My sons thought otherwise, and they snaked and weaved their way through the people. Somehow, we kept up with them; and when we made it into the room that housed the famed work of art, there were our two boys, standing in front of the *Mona Lisa* with grins on their faces. It was much smaller than expected, but we felt a large victory in finding it!

I don't know what came over me, but after we returned home I had an intense desire to go to the Holy Land. I had no idea how I would get there, especially on the heels of the extravagant trip we had just taken to Europe. Knowing the timing was not right, I still prayed one day in my car, "L-RD, would you provide a way for me to go to Israel, the land of my ancestors and the children of the promise?"

The following week, I was listening to a Messianic Rabbi give his testimony of how he became a believer in Yeshua. It was a fascinating account of how he was addicted to pot, worked a dead-end job in real estate sales in San Antonio, Texas, and became fed up with his life. One day he decided to throw his drugs out the window and asked Yeshua to save him. That is when this man, born and raised in a Jewish household, had his encounter with Yeshua, and he was never the same after that.

When he finished telling his story, I said to the bearded rabbi, "I love your testimony—not only because you are now a Jewish believer in Yeshua, but because all this happened in my home town of San Antonio." His response caught me off guard: "When is the last time you went to Israel?" I said, "I've never been to Israel." He answered, "I don't think anyone should be in ministry if they've never been to Israel. How would you like to go with me and a group of pastors to the Holy Land in December—for half price?"

December 2014 was only a few months away, but I remembered my prayer in the car the week before, and I believed *ADONAI* was presenting an opportunity on a golden platter—for half the cost! What would my husband Jeff, a financial guy, say? Would he ask me to jump through a lot of hoops in order to go? I immediately prayed that if I was supposed to travel with this group to the Holy Land, Jeff would respond with a simple "Okay," and that would be my sign to proceed.

I made the phone call to Jeff and explained what happened. In an effort to sweeten the deal, I did tell him this trip could constitute both my Christmas and birthday presents. "Can I go?" Then my husband responded, "Okay." "Okay?" No strings attached? No question about how we were going to pay for it? Well, okay! I began making plans to travel to Israel in early December.

A few months later, I attended an event where I sat with a friend of mine who is prophetic. She often managed tours to Israel, and I excitedly told her about my upcoming trip. Just as the event speaker began to share, she turned and looked at me with intensity in her eyes and said, "I have a word for you." She couldn't give it to me at that moment because the presenter was beginning his message, so

I had to sit in anticipation throughout the rest of the event. I couldn't even focus on what the speaker was saying.

Afterward, overwhelmed by curiosity, I asked, "Well? What is the word?"

She said, "The Host has invited you to Israel, and He has a message for you there." "The Host? The L-RD of Hosts?"

The one and the same, *ADONAI* Tzva'ot.

According to One for Israel, a Jewish ministry, "When we call our Heavenly Father the 'L-RD of Hosts,' there is so much in that name. Yes, there are the myriad armies of angels at His disposal, and yes, He is a warrior, mighty in battle; but He is also the conductor of the beautiful orchestra that is the entirety of all creation. Every atom, every molecule, moves in accordance with His purposes and at His command. He sustains everything by His powerful word."[xi]

You can find this name of G-d throughout the Old Testament, but especially In Isaiah 8–10 when *ADONAI* referred to himself as *ADONAI* Tzva'ot numerous times when pronouncing impending judgment on the people of Judah through an Assyrian invasion. In Isaiah 8:13 *ADONAI* Tzva'ot says it is He the people should fear, and that He is the one who makes them holy. In Isaiah 8:18 the prophet Isaiah tells us *ADONAI* Tzva'ot dwells in His Temple on Mount Zion, from where He issues signs and warnings. Isaiah 9:6–7 provides a prophecy about the coming Messiah, Yeshua, who will rule with fairness and justice from the throne of His ancestor David for all eternity. Isaiah 9:7 says it's the zeal of the L-RD of Hosts that will accomplish this. But following the Assyrian invasion, the L-RD of Hosts also pronounces judgment on Assyria. In Isaiah 10:24–25, He says that His anger against Judah will subside and then that anger, in turn, will rise up and destroy the Assyrians. All of this tells me it's *ADONAI* Tzva'ot who is in control, and He has a plan.

Even though I had no idea what my message from *ADONAI* Tzva'ot would entail, I knew by using this term, the L-RD was in charge of my future as well. I knew all the reminders about my Jewish father and Jewish roots, the celebration of Jewish holidays with friends, and this feeling of being "Jewish," even though I was told I did not qualify, would all come together in some way on this excursion overseas.

I entered an attitude of prayer from the moment I received this prophetic word to the time I boarded the plane bound for Israel, and throughout my stay in the land of my ancestors, Abraham, Isaac and Jacob. I prayed that I would not miss YHWH's message and that *ADONAI* would highlight the correspondence so I would know it was from Him when I heard it.

After an eleven-hour flight, we finally landed in the Promised Land. We checked into the hotel, and then our first stop was Arial, Israel, where the Biblical Gardens are located. The Biblical Gardens provide a miniature overview of the history of Israel. It was a great way to get a broad understanding about where this journey with G-d began and where the

Israelites wandered in those early years of an on-again-off-again allegiance to *ADONAI*. Also at the Biblical Gardens was a replica of the first Tabernacle, originally constructed in Gilgal after the conquest and division of the land. The Tabernacle, or Tent of Meeting, which housed the Ark of the Covenant where G-d resided, was later moved to Shiloh. It was the center of the Israelite's worship for 369 years.xii

I purchased one of my favorite necklaces when our tour visited Shiloh. It is a silver pendant with the Tabernacle displayed on it, and it falls directly on my heart. It is a Christian's belief that as a result of a relationship with Yeshua, G-d's Spirit now resides in our heart. It's His new dwelling place. For me, it's also a daily reminder of the love relationship I have with my heavenly Father.

However, the image that spoke to me the most at the Biblical Gardens was an olive tree, highlighted with a bright spotlight pointing upward from its base. I wondered if this was symbolic of *ADONAI*'s gift that He would present to me at some point on this trip. I admired the olive tree's beauty; and as my gaze locked into this native tree of Israel, it was as if G-d was saying another Shema: "Listen! Pay attention to the olive tree." *Would my message have something to do with the olive tree?*

I was an attentive student, tuning my ears into the gentle whisper of G-d, like the one Elijah heard when he was on the run trying to escape an angry King Ahab and Queen Jezebel. That dangerous duo wanted to kill G-d's prophet after he made a fool of and wiped out 450 false prophets of Baal. Elijah, tuckered out from running, made it a far as Beersheba, where he sat down under a broom bush and prayed that he might die. In his depression, he fell asleep before being awakened by an angel—twice—who told him to eat. He would need sustenance to be strong enough for what was about to occur at his next stop, Horeb, a forty-day journey. Horeb, also known as Mount Sinai, was the mountain where Moses met with G-d, got a glimpse of His glory, and received the Ten Commandments. Now G-d was about to make a cameo appearance with Elijah, because He knew His servant needed a pick-me-up. Here's what happened:

Then he said, "Come out and stand on the mount before *ADONAI*." Behold, *ADONAI* was passing by—a great and mighty wind was tearing at the mountains and shattering cliffs before *ADONAI*. But *ADONAI* was not in the wind. After the wind there was an earthquake, but *ADONAI* was not in the earthquake. After the earthquake a fire, but *ADONAI* was not in the fire. After the fire there was a soft whisper of a voice. As soon as Elijah heard it, he wrapped his face in his mantle, went out and stood at the entrance of the cave (1 King 19:11-13).

Then Elijah received his detailed instruction from G-d. He told him to go back the way he came and anoint two kings to replace Ahab—Hazael over Aram and Jehu over Israel. There was a new plan in place, and Ahab and Jezebel's days were numbered. Knowing Elijah may have been experiencing holy burnout, G-d also told him to anoint Elisha to replace him as prophet. At that point, Elijah had to realize G-d was with him. What if he hadn't been in a position to listen, too busy to hear from his Maker?

Oh, please let me hear your gentle whisper, L-RD.

I continued to lean into each stop in case *ADONAI* decided to speak as He had whispered to Elijah. From Ariel, we spent time in Nazareth, the childhood home of Yeshua, and Magdala, a first-century fishing town and the hometown of Mary Magdalene, who was possessed with seven demons until Yeshua cast them out (Luke 8:2). We also took a boat ride on the Sea of Galilee with a group of Sri Lankan believers. We could not understand each other, but we connected through the international language of dance, as we joyously danced to the traditional Jewish song, "Hava Nagila.*"* I will never be asked to appear on the television program *So You Think You Can Dance.* Despite my athleticism, I've always been clumsy and was a little worried I'd lose my balance on the rocky Sea of Galilee. Surprisingly, I got through this classic with flying colors.

I had an intimate moment with Yeshua on the Mount of Beatitudes, where Yeshua delivered the famous "Sermon on the Mount" found in Matthew 5. We were given about ten minutes of quiet time, so I took the opportunity to pray the Beatitudes over myself. *Help me, Lisa, to be poor in spirit, O G-d. I pray that I will be meek. Enable me to hunger and thirst for righteousness. Show me how to be merciful like you are. I want to be pure in heart so I can see you, G-d. Teach me how to be a peacemaker.* When I completed my prayer, I looked up, and the clouds formed a shape that looked like Yeshua. There was a man in a robe, with his arms outstretched. It was too perfectly defined to be random. By the time it occurred to me to snap a photo, the image had already dissipated. It lasted only a second and was put together especially for me. I believe G-d had heard the heart of my prayers and provided a supernatural affirmation.

I still had no specific message, however; but as the theaters boldly advertise, it was "coming soon!" Appropriately, the powerful correspondence that had been prophesied months before would be delivered in the central hub of Israel, Old Town Jerusalem.

The setting was a gift store called Shorashim, which means "Roots" in English. The business is located in the Jewish Quarter and run by a Jewish scholar and transplant from Canada, Moshe Avraham Kempinski. Kempinski's heart is to educate visitors and create better relations between the Jewish people and the rest of the world; so when tour groups visit his shop, he takes moments to teach about the history of Israel. Kempinski has written books, like *The Heart of the People and Accessing Inner Joy: Insights into the Biblical Festivals.* He also has a theory about visitors like myself. He maintains that "Nobody comes to Israel without being invited by G-d. And though people may not know what drew them here, they know it is not meant to be another beach vacation on the Riviera."[xiii] This line of thinking was a confirmation of the prophetic word I received months before this visit. I had been issued a divine invitation with a golden seal, stamped in heaven.

Once we were inside Shorashim, Kempinski locked the door to his store so he'd have our undivided attention with no interruptions, and he had us sit down on the floor before he began to speak. As he shared about the roots of Israel, you could feel the passion and heart he had for his country, and he wanted us to understand about this land that was special to *ADONAI*.

At some point in the short lecture, he asked, "Do any of you know the meaning of the olive tree?" I did not, but my eyebrows raised because I remembered the brightly lit olive tree that the Holy Spirit had highlighted in the Biblical Gardens. I locked in as Kempinski continued speaking.

"The leaves of the olive tree represent G-d's protective covering over His people.

"But in order to get the fruit off the tree, you have to thresh it, and that represents G-d's discipline in our lives.

"The trunk of the olive tree lives many years; it has a life expectancy of around 800 years."

Then it felt like there was a moment of pause for a holy drum roll to accentuate what He would say next. *ADONAI* was issuing a type of Shema: "Listen Lisa!" So I was even more attentive as Kempinski concluded this story about the olive tree.

"However, the roots of the olive tree *never* die."

And that is when time stood still and the gentle whisper of G-d entered the room.

Lisa, your Jewish father died, but your Jewish roots never died.

It was the soft, still voice that Elijah heard. I sat motionless as I meditated on this message, the message that G-d brought me over 7,000 miles across the Atlantic Ocean to receive. *ADONAI* had issued the word about my Jewish roots at a shop ironically named "Roots." Only He could write a script like that. But what was I supposed to do with it? What did it mean? Where would it lead? It would take two years for the answers to begin to unfold.

Thinking the rest of the trip would be anticlimactic compared to that moment with *ADONAI,* I was surprised when G-d added an exclamation point to my Israel experience. It was another miracle that occurred as I overcame one of my greatest fears.

It happened on the Mount of Olives overlooking Jerusalem. A camel named Kojak was at the overlook, standing stately, and his handler must have thought I was an easy sell. He focused on me and said, "Come on, Mama. Why don't you ride the camel, Mama? When you do, we'll take a photo so you can show your friends back home." You see, because my father died on a horse, I was raised to be afraid of horses. My grandmother Nonnie would often say, "You're not riding horses, are you?" She was fearful that I would suffer the same fate as my dad if I ever rode a horse; so by the time I was an adult, I had a debilitating fear of horses, and the equines I came into contact with knew it.

While a camel is not exactly a horse, it's still an animal you ride—and it is even taller than a horse! I sized Kojak up and had no interest in getting up close and personal with him. However, the handler was relentless, and I began to soften my stance. I had observed that Kojak crouched down so people could hop on his back, which made it easier, and I thought, *Okay, I can do this, but only for a minute.*

So with great trepidation, I sat on Kojak, and I'm sure he felt the adrenaline that was running at full tilt throughout my body. Making it to this point was a major milestone, and it was enough for me to pose for a quick pic, holding tightly to the reins. Then the handler pushed the limit a little further. He said, "Come on, Mama. Take your hands off the reins, Mama. We'll snap a picture you can show your friends back home!" What? I was worried if I took my hands off the reins, the camel would bolt over the guardrail at the Mount of Olives, straight into the Kidron Valley below.

But that day, with strength that could have only come from above, I decided there was no better place to overcome one of my greatest fears than the site in Israel where Yeshua once ascended and will one day return again. I let go of the reins, raised my arms high in the air, and praised the Only one who can help us overcome our greatest fears and troubled past, *ADONAI*. In addition to my message from the L-RD of Hosts, this was a memory I will never forget as long as I live.

I found that miracles happen in this special land called Israel. Now I had to figure out what to do with the direct message I had received earlier from *ADONAI* concerning my Jewish roots—roots that had just risen from the dead.

Chapter 4
The Search

On the plane ride home, I spent many sleepless hours reflecting about this word from *ADONAI*, and I had many questions for Him. Being a former reporter who desires to know something about everything, I always have a bucketful of questions about a variety of subjects. My husband often exclaims, "You ask too many questions!" But these inquiries had to do with the divine word I had received at the shop in the Jewish Quarter.

"What do you want me to do?

"Should I take Hebrew?"

"Should I attend a Messianic synagogue?"

I was in a "need-to-know" mode and quizzed my heavenly Father about next steps. There was no immediate answer. I thought, *How can the L-RD put this in my lap, then not provide the instruction manual?* So in my "can-do," rather than "wait-on-G-d" fashion, I explored possibilities.

There was a Messianic synagogue that rented space from our church on Saturday's. How convenient! I attended one Saturday and liked it. I thought the Rabbi was a gifted speaker, but the service was longer than expected. I remember looking at my watch and thinking, *Wow! We are two hours in with no sign of the service ending.* Then there was Jewish training all afternoon. In addition to my church responsibilities on Sunday, this would take me away from my family on a day when my youngest son was home from school, and I was not willing to give up that much time. It also seemed odd that most of the people who attended this synagogue had no Jewish roots at all. When the rabbi found out I actually had a Jewish father, he reached out to me regularly, inviting me to classes and events they were holding at their congregation. It was obvious he wanted more people with Jewish blood in his congregation. However, I did not have peace about moving forward; so after trying to take matters in my own hands, all I could do was wait for G-d to speak again.

Meanwhile, I never took a Hebrew class, but I still have an overwhelming desire to study Old Testament Hebrew. At the writing of this book, I have signed up to begin working on my Doctor of Ministry in Messianic Studies at The King's University, and one of the requirements is to take Hebrew 1 and 2. I am praying this old brain will be able to grasp the ancient language.

The Bible says a day is like a thousand years to the L-RD, and a thousand years are like one day

(2 Peter 3:8), so my next steps did not come in the time frame I would have chosen. It was a full two years after my trip to the Holy Land that *ADONAI* started making His chess moves. Both my husband and I began to feel like He wanted us to leave our church. It had been our home for eleven years. I co-founded a women's ministry there, was women's ministry leader for four years, and taught Bible study at this church. My husband served at the denomination's conference level in Finance and Administration. I had a seminary degree from this denomination. We loved our friends in our Sunday school class. We were entrenched, and leaving at this point didn't make sense; but we were seeing the church stray away from the inerrancy of the Word of G-d, and I clearly heard more of a firm tone from the Holy Spirit, rather than a whisper this time. He asked, "Who are you going to align with during these last days?"

Many of us believe that Yeshua is going to return one day, and all believers will be "raptured" from earth and taken with Yeshua to Heaven, not seeing a physical death. I believe this because it's clearly laid out in the Bible and because of a prophetic word I received twenty years ago.

I was living in San Antonio, and one morning I was barely awake when I heard an audible voice say, "There's still more to do. The year is 204?." The reason there is a question mark is because I didn't catch the last number. I asked the Holy Spirit to repeat Himself; He didn't, but He got His point across. I knew it wasn't my thought, because the only

45

intelligent thought I can muster up that early in the morning is *I need coffee*. If it had been my rumination, I also would have had a definitive year, rather than leave it open-ended. This prophetic word told me time is short before Yeshua's return, and He has some jobs for me to do. The apostle Paul speaks about this day in 1 Corinthians 15:51–52: "Behold, I tell you a mystery: We shall not all sleep, but we shall all be changed— in a moment, in the twinkling of an eye, at the last shofar. For the shofar will sound, and the dead will be raised incorruptible, and we will be changed."

Yeshua HaMashiach also painted a picture of this future event in Matthew 24:

For just as the days of Noah were, so will be the coming of the Son of Man. For in those days before the flood, they were eating and drinking, marrying and giving in marriage, until the day Noah entered the ark. And they did not understand until the flood came and swept them all away. So shall it be at the coming of the Son of Man. Then two men will be in the field, one taken and one left. Two women will be grinding at the mill, one taken and one left. Therefore stay alert; for you do not know what day your L-RD is coming. But know this, that if the master of the house had known what time the thief was coming, he would have kept watch and not let his house be broken into. So you also must be ready, for the Son of Man is coming at an hour you do not expect (Matthew 24:37–44).

I have shared my faith openly with one of my dear Jewish friends, who to-date still doesn't believe

Yeshua is the promised Messiah, yet she is willing to listen. One day I said, "If my husband and I disappear, and there's an inexplicable disappearance of millions around the world, it means Yeshua has returned. Will you believe then?" She responded with a laugh, "Yes, I will believe."

So as difficult as the move was from one church to another, we needed to be obedient and align ourselves elsewhere. We began to visit other congregations and ventured out of our denomination. We started with our community first but couldn't find a church that we both agreed on. However, we kept returning to a mega-church called Gateway Church in Southlake, Texas. We thought the preaching by Senior Pastors Robert Morris and Jimmy Evans was exceptional. I especially loved the worship and was overwhelmed by emotion when I saw scores of men and women raising their hands to praise *ADONAI* in the sanctuary. I felt like I had been unleashed. I had raised my hand on occasion at our old church, but it was a wimpy arm raise because I was too worried about what people would think. In retrospect, I realize it is *ADONAI* we should please—not people.

Praise is an important aspect in our relationship with the L-RD. Throughout the Psalms, you can see that King David understood the importance of worship; but there are many other examples of worship found throughout the Torah, the Prophets, and the Writings.

After the Israelites saw the mighty hand of the L-RD displayed against the Egyptians when He parted the Red Sea, Moses and his sister Miriam lifted up a song of praise: "I will sing to *ADONAI*, for He is highly exalted! The horse and its rider He has thrown into the sea. *ADONAI* is my strength and song, and He has become my salvation. This is my God, and I will glorify Him, my father's God, and I will exalt Him" (Exodus 15:1–2).

Once Nehemiah and his fellow workers completed rebuilding the walls of Jerusalem, there was a huge celebration with the reading of the Word and praise at the center. According to Nehemiah 12, the Israelites celebrated with songs of thanksgiving and with the music of cymbals, harps and lyres. There were two large choirs assembled to give thanks. According to Nehemiah 12:43, "The joy in Jerusalem could be heard from far off."

When the king of Judah, King Jehoshaphat, heard that enemy armies where approaching, his battle cry was worship. He had a group of singers walk ahead of his army, singing and praising the L-RD for His holy splendor. They sang, "Praise *ADONAI*, for His mercy endures forever" (2 Chronicles 20:21). At the very moment they sang and gave praise, the opposing armies of Ammon, Moab, and Mount Seir began fighting among themselves and destroyed each other.

Worship brings us into the presence of *ADONAI*, and it has power.

In order to move to this new house of worship, I had to overcome my stereotypical feelings about mega-churches. And I did not like congregations where family members seemed to be in control. However, I found out this church is governed by a

48

board of elders, and I also had a change of heart about families serving in leadership ministry together. I came to the realization that it is admirable when children desire to follow their parents into the same vocation. I also wanted the leadership to be authentic and more concerned about the spiritual well-being of their members, rather than church growth, which I found to be true of the pastors I met.

Still not entirely convinced, I threw up other roadblocks. This church location was a much further distance from our home than our old congregation was. We used to get to church in less than ten minutes' time, and this one was thirty-five minutes away. I was concerned about driving those miles every weekend. If we got involved through service, we'd be going back and forth even more, taking up a large chunk of time. However, one day when we were visiting, there was a man stationed at one of the sanctuary entrances wearing a pastor's badge. I shared that we were thinking about joining but told him about my worries over the long drive. He said, "Well, I drive almost two hours every weekend from Wichita Falls." I knew where Wichita Falls was, having spent some time there covering the Dallas Cowboys' training camp. When he said that, I thought, *I guess a half-hour is not that bad.* I never saw that pastor again, and I still wonder if *ADONAI* placed an angel at the sanctuary door that day to gently direct us to Gateway.

While I was still pondering what to do, there was one service when Gateway had a guest speaker, Christine Caine. Christine is an international speaker and founder of A21 Ministries, an outreach that combats human trafficking. She was sharing about her own journey when G-d moved her from one church to her Australian mega-church, Hillsong. In her unforgettable Aussie accent, she said the Holy Spirit spoke to her about the move and repeatedly whispered, "If you want to be there, you have to be here. If you want to be there, you have to be here." I then felt in my spirit, *Lisa, if you want to be there, you have to be here.* I asked myself, *Why do I have to be here?* At the time I thought *there* meant a new level spiritually. I had no clue that this could have something to do with my return to Jewish roots. I thought, *If I have to be here, then my Lutheran-born-and-bred husband who has his hands in his pockets during worship will have to lead the way.* A few weeks later, my husband grabbed a new member card out of the seat pocket in front of us, and said, "Don't we need to fill this out?"

So we joined Gateway Church. What I didn't know—but what G-d obviously had foreknowledge of at the time—was that Gateway believes "to the Jew first," gives its first tithe to Israel, and has a Jewish ministry and a monthly Shabbat service. "To the Jew first" means that the Gospel, salvation through Yeshua, was presented to the Jews first, then to the Gentiles. Paul talks about this concept in Romans 1:16 when he said, "For I am not ashamed of the Good News, for it is the power of G-d for salvation to everyone who trusts—to the Jew first and also to the Greek." The ministry One for Israel explains this concept further: "You have been made 'one new man' with the Jewish people, you have been given the same access in the same Spirit to the same Father (thanks to the same Messiah) and you are fellow citizens – a member of the household of G-d along with the people of Israel. You are no longer strangers, but part of the commonwealth of Israel. The dividing wall that once stood in the Temple court, beyond which only Jewish people could enter, has gone. Gentiles are not second class in any way—thanks to Yeshua, we all now have equal access to the G-d of Israel, the Father of us all."[xiv]

G-d led us *there* to Gateway Church and wanted us to take this first leap of faith, before he did the big reveal.

For different reasons, the L-RD had taken both of us to the perfect place where we could grow spiritually and where I could acquire more knowledge about my Hebraic roots that were sprouting more and more every day. My husband and I began attending the monthly Shabbat services. It was fun! There were dancers in the front, and we sang the "Shema" at the beginning. There was a reading of the Torah and a message from the Torah. When I was in town, it became a regular appointment on my calendar.

I also started attending a weekly Havdalah teaching presented by Dr. Greg Stone, the pastoral leader of Jewish Ministries. Dr. Stone, as mentioned earlier, is a Messianic Jew whose parents were both Jewish. He attended Hebrew school on Sundays and Wednesdays from first grade until his Bar Mitzvah. He participated in youth groups at two local synagogues and graduated from Hebrew high school.

He took private Bible lessons with a staff Rabbi because he was considering becoming a Rabbi.

But these worthy plans took a sharp turn when he was in high school. Dr. Stone says, "When I was a senior in high school, I started smoking marijuana. When I went off to college, I became addicted to marijuana, and then to cocaine. My life fell apart due to a serious addiction and I dropped out of college. My dad suggested that I join the Air Force, saying, 'It will make a man of you.'"

He continues, "While in the Air Force, I was befriended by an Air Force pilot who invited me to church. I went, and the love of the people seemed very real. I did not know I needed to make a decision to receive Yeshua; but the tangible love was so real that I really wanted what the people had, so I made an appointment to see the youth pastor five days after the church visit." That decision was life-changing.

After his stint in the Air Force, Pastor Greg Stone entered the ministry. Now Dr. Stone teaches and speaks all over the world, and one of the many responsibilities he has is to provide teaching about Jewish roots through the Havdalah class.

For the non-Jewish readers of this book, "Havdalah" is a word that means "separation." It represents the end of the Shabbat in which the holy day is separated from the mundane day that follows. There is a lighting of candles, and blessings recited over spices and wine or grape juice. In our class, this all happens prior to the teaching.

Havdalah also became a regular part of my week. Pastor Stone taught on a number of subjects; but when he decided to go through the book of Revelation, which includes prophetic words about the days to come, I asked if he would like a prayer covering during that stretch of teaching. Revelation is a book that speaks not only about Yeshua's return, but also about a millennial kingdom and the eventual destruction of evil. I had participated in a Revelation study before this one. We never finished it because two of the couples in the group had a falling out. I later realized we had some spiritual opposition, because the enemy of our souls did not want us studying about his demise.

So Pastor Stone agreed to have me form a prayer team for the Havdalah class after I went through Altar Ministry and group training, and we put a group of intercessors together who began praying regularly for that class. That led to an invitation to be the volunteer intercessory prayer leader for the overall Jewish Ministries; and to this day, I am still serving in that position.

One distinct message I received from Dr. Stone's teaching is that the book of Revelation, which speaks of the end of days as we know it, is a very *Jewish* book. He provided two quotes from *The Jewish Annotated New Testament,* written by Jewish scholars who serve at Oxford. None of the editors are believers in Yeshua. However they say the following: "Revelation shows no sense of a Christianity, or even of a Jewish-devotion, unmoored from Judaism."[xv] "Increasingly, scholars are looking at Revelation as a

Jewish text that reveals a heavenly Christ rather than a Christian text with Jewish attributes."[xvi]. Dr. Stone says, "The book of Revelation is full of Jewish thinking and typology. It cannot be understood apart from a Jewish grid of comprehension."

Yeshua is Jewish. His twelve disciples were Jewish. They observed Jewish holidays, and many of the first believers were Jewish, although many Jews rejected Jesus at the time. Yeshua came to this earth to provide the chosen ones relief from all of the tedious sins offerings they had to perform, as He, the Lamb of G-d, would be the perfect sacrifice for their sins, and so we, through the covering of His blood, could be seen as "righteous" and "clean" in *ADONAI*'s eyes. The Bible, a very Jewish book, contained a message of salvation for the Jews; but in the midst of rejection, G-d made a way for the Gentiles to receive this same gift. Gentiles have been accepted into G-d's special family through Yeshua's sacrificial offering.

If the Jewish people had not preserved the Holy Scriptures, we would not have the Torah, the Prophets, and the Writings that make up the entire Old Testament. Many of us rely on G-d's word for inspiration and direction, and because of that I am grateful for its preservation throughout the years.

What I have also learned through Messianic ministry is that just because you are a believer in Yeshua, you don't stop being "Jewish." Sometimes you become even more knowledgeable about Judaism than you ever were before.

My Jewish friend Donna was in management for a chain of health clubs and was about to quit the best job she ever had, when her boss began to talk to her about purpose. That was part of her problem. She did not know what her purpose in life was. He told her we are all created by G-d for a purpose, but in order to know that purpose we have to be right with Him. He then asked her if she had ever sinned. She said, "No sir, I don't believe so." She thought of sin as the great big sins like murder and stealing, which is the way a lot of people think today. Then he asked her, "Have you ever wanted something that someone else had?" "Well, yes," she said. Her boss went on: "That is coveting; and the Ten Commandments clearly say, 'Thou shall not covet,' so that makes you a sinner. And G-d cannot be in the presence of sin—it separates us from Him. So that is why He had to send His Son Yeshua as a sacrifice to bridge the gap between Himself and mankind, so we could one day live in heaven with Him forever. Do you want to be separated from G-d forever, or live with Him forever? If you want to be assured of living in eternity with Him, you can pray a prayer to receive Yeshua; and if you do that, I promise, you never give up being Jewish."

That day, Donna acknowledged she was a sinner and that Yeshua died on the cross as a perfect sacrifice for her sins, that He rose from the dead and sits at the right hand of G-d the Father. She gave her heart to Yeshua and felt a physical sensation of her heart melting. She is now leading a successful Dallas-based ministry called Roaring Lambs.

Unlike Donna and other Messianic Jewish friends of mine, my story is more unique. It's about a rediscovering of Jewish tradition and holidays, understanding the Jewishness of the Bible, and doing my own investigation of what my people may have missed about Yeshua in the ancient Scriptures. This treasure hunt would unearth some gems that proved to me that Yeshua was part of G-d's plan from the beginning.

Chapter 5
The Traditions

Since my Jewish father was not a part of my life, I did not grow up celebrating or observing any of the traditional Jewish holidays or traditions until I was an adult. I became aware of Passover Seders after we became close friends with our Jewish neighbors in San Antonio, and just this year I finally bought a Seder plate. After I had my "aha moment" in Israel, I became more cognizant of *all* the festivals. I now check the calendar to see when Rosh Hashanah falls. I bought a Menorah to use for celebrating the eight days of Hanukkah; however, I can never seem to get the candles to fit right. (You'd think they'd create universal candles that worked with the Menorah candle holders.) I observe Yom Kippur. And I am aware of the Feast of Tabernacles (also known as the Festival of Booths). This tradition, called "Sukkot" in Hebrew, was commanded by *ADONAI* in Leviticus 23. G-d wanted the Israelites to observe Sukkot by living in temporary shelters for seven days as a reminder that when their ancestors were in the wilderness, He provided them booths to dwell in. The Feast of Tabernacles is also a time of rejoicing, because it's a remembrance that when the harvest season was over, G-d provided more than enough food for His people to survive.

Many Jews today celebrate this holiday by building their own booth, or sukkah, a four-sided, temporary structure, with palm branches for the open roof, and sometimes canvas for the walls. For the seven days of this holiday, many observant families eat their meals there, and others go so far as to sleep in this temporary dwelling as well.[xvii]

However, this is the one tradition I still need to embrace, because I have an aversion to camping. Years ago, I finally gave in to our friends' numerous attempts at coaxing me to go on a group camping trip. My attire on arrival gave everyone a good laugh. I came in wearing full jewelry, my leather coat, a nice sweater and leggings. What's wrong with that? I was there, wasn't I? This may have been when my husband Jeff first started calling me a "Jewish princess." Jeff and I struggled to put up our tent, but we were finally able to get it done; and after a delicious dinner around the campfire and the sharing of many stories and a few jokes, it was time to retire. *I just might get used to this camping thing after all.*

However, in the middle of the night we experienced the mother of all thunderstorms, ahead of a strong cold front. It was October (ironically, the month of Sukkot), and the storm woke me up. I then realized I needed a bathroom, and it was an emergency. I tried to talk myself back to sleep, but it was no use. The more I willed myself to go to sleep, the more wide-awake I became. I knew what I had to do. I had to brave the walk, in a downpour, in the pitch-black night to the facilities, which seemed to be a mile away. In reality, they were only about 500 feet from the tent, but I was scared—I was concerned about the critters that might be lurking around—and I was cold.

Needless to say, we never went camping again. My idea of camping is staying in a Hilton on a beach; and fortunately, my husband has the same mindset. But know this, if *ADONAI* calls me to live in a temporary booth one day, I'll do it! I just hope there's a porta-potty nearby.

Taking a Shabbat rest is another mainstay of Judaism, and it's taken me many years to finally understand the importance of pausing weekly from work, as *ADONAI* commanded: "Remember *Yom Shabbat*, to keep it holy" (Exodus 20:8). At this point I need to confess: *Hello, I'm Lisa Burkhardt Worley, and I am a workaholic.* But our heavenly Father did not design us to go non-stop 24-7 without a break. I am thankful that through His mercy, He didn't zap me for many years of violating this important commandment.

There was no such mercy in ancient times, as seen in Numbers 15:32–36: "While *Bnei-Yisrael* were in the wilderness, they found a man gathering wood on the *Shabbat*. Those who found him gathering wood brought him to Moses, Aaron and the entire assembly. They kept him under arrest, not being clear what was to be done to him. *ADONAI* said to Moses, "The man has to die. The whole assembly is to stone him with stones outside the camp." So the whole assembly took him outside the camp. They stoned him with stones. He died just as *ADONAI* commanded Moses."

This punishment seems a little over the top; but in his book, *Take the Day Off,* my pastor Robert Morris says, "But we have to keep in mind that the laws that Moses delivered to the Israelites were designed for their benefit *and* to assure the success of His grand plan of redemption. Those laws contained principles for remaining healthy as individuals and families and strong as a society. G-d understood what we clearly do not. Namely, that a society in which people work seven days a week is just as vulnerable to collapse as a society in which people are free to rape and murder without consequences. G-d was crafting a culture and a people that could survive and thrive so that in the fullness of time, His only begotten Son could enter the world through them."

So after many repeated messages from *ADONAI,* culminating with a health scare, I began taking a Shabbat rest. Someone once said, "On the Sabbath, do with your mind what you would normally do with your hands, or vice-versa." I use my mind a lot during the week, so on my Sabbath, I work in the yard, exercise, or play golf with my husband. Sometimes I even take a nap. What I've found is that taking a Shabbat rest has led to more productivity in the other six days of my week. This book is an example, as it's come together in about four months. I believe *ADONAI* is blessing my decision to finally put work aside for twenty-four hours; and I am now, as my kids like to say, "chill-axing."

The observance that I seem to connect with the most, however, is Passover. There's something about the symbolism in Pesach that speaks to me. After G-d brought on plague after plague in an effort to convince Pharaoh to set the Israelites free after 400 years of slavery, it wasn't until the final plague, the death of the firstborn, that Pharaoh finally relented. In this horrific scenario, *ADONAI* passed over all of Egypt and killed the firstborn child in every household. If the Israelites did not protect their homes, they would fall victim to this plague as well.

In order to assure their safety, the Israelites had to slaughter a one-year-old male lamb without defect and place its blood on the sides and tops of the doorframes of their houses. Then there were more instructions in Exodus 12: "That same night they are to eat the meat roasted over the fire, along with bitter herbs, and bread made without yeast. Do not eat the meat raw or boiled in water, but roast it over a fire— with the head, legs and internal organs. Do not leave any of it till morning; if some is left till morning, you must burn it. This is how you are to eat it: with your cloak tucked into your belt, your sandals on your feet and your staff in your hand. Eat it in haste; it is the LORD's Passover" (Exodus 12:8-11, NIV).

That night, G-d passed through Egypt and struck down every firstborn of both people and animals, and brought judgment on all the gods of Egypt.

When He saw the blood over the Israelites' doors, He passed over their houses. He then said, "This is a day you are to commemorate; for the generations to come you shall celebrate it as a festival to the LORD—a lasting ordinance" (Exodus 12:14).

According to the instructions for Pesach, you are also supposed to fast from leavened bread; so for the first time ever, this Passover I ate no bread with yeast in it, and I also gave up pork. I had toyed with the idea of going completely Kosher every day of the year, but I decided to eat Kosher just on the Jewish holidays, instead. It seemed like the right decision for me.

After sharing with my spiritual daughter Lara my urgency to write this book, she asked, "I'm wondering, did this idea for the book come after you fasted from leaven during Passover?" Lara came into my life years ago when she worked for me, post-television, in public relations at the San Antonio International Airport. When her mother passed away, I believe I heard *ADONAI* say, "She's your daughter now." After job stints in Chicago and New York, she now lives close by, and I try to be a spiritual mother to her. Now my more spiritually mature daughter was opening my eyes to something I had not seen.

I answered her question: "Yes, I felt called to write this book after my fast." I realized when we fast from something out of reverence for G-d, we can often hear His voice more clearly and it can result in a directional shift.

Passover this year was unusual, because it fell in the midst of the Coronavirus pandemic that brought the world to a standstill. As I write this chapter, we are emerging from a stay-at-home order, but we're still not out of the woods. For a while, I didn't know anyone with COVID-19, but now I know several who've contracted it. Fortunately, they've all either recovered or are doing well.

Sue, a prophetic friend who serves as a leader on our Jewish Ministries prayer team at church, said prior to this year's Passover, "I have received a word that we need to anoint our doors with oil, because the Angel of Death is going to pass over our homes; if we anoint our doors, we'll be safe. She asked me to write a teaching on this to share with our team. So after I obediently anointed all openings to our home, I wrote the following:

The Healing Power of Anointing

What are you doing so the Coronavirus will "pass over" you during this trying season? Social distancing? Self-quarantining? Lots of vitamins?

The observance of the first Passover is less than three weeks away. The original Passover occurred almost 3,500 years ago when G-d demonstrated His mighty power through ten different plagues. The plagues eventually convinced the Pharaoh of Egypt to release the Israelites from slavery and allow them to return to their land. It took a horrific final plague, the death of the Egyptians' firstborn children, for Pharaoh to relent and free G-d's people.

Meanwhile, the Israelites were spared from loss because they painted blood from an unblemished lamb over their door frames, causing G-d to "pass over" their homes during this last plague. Therefore,

Jews worldwide, many with Jewish roots like myself, and a number of Gentiles observe Passover to this day, in thankfulness for G-d's mercy toward them.

Today, I don't have blood over my door frames, but I do have a Mezuzah on the front door that carries the words of Deuteronomy 6:4-9 (NIV): "Hear, O Israel: The LORD our God, the LORD is one. Love the LORD your God with all your heart and with all your soul and with all your strength. These commandments that I give you today are to be on your hearts. Impress them on your children. Talk about them when you sit at home and when you walk along the road, when you lie down and when you get up. Tie them as symbols on your hands and bind them on your foreheads. Write them on the door frames of your houses and on your gates." I have those words posted on the door to my garage as well. I don't want to ever forget the most important thing I need to do each day—to love G-d with everything I have in me—every breath, every thought, and every word. I also desire G-d's protection over our home, so I physically cover it in this way.

But in light of the Coronavirus pandemic, I am taking the concept a step further. On Thursday, I anointed the door frame of my home with oil—the "oil of gladness," to be exact. Anointing something or someone with oil did not end with Old-Testament times. In Mark 6:13, the disciples were "driving out many demons and anointing with oil many who were sick and healing them." James 5:14 (NIV) says, "Is anyone among you sick? Let them call the elders of the church to pray over them and anoint them with oil in the name of the LORD." In Exodus 40:9 G-d told the Israelites to anoint the tabernacle with oil.

The Spirit of G-d used to reside in the tabernacle, a physical structure, but where does He reside today? We are His tabernacle if we have accepted Yeshua, the unblemished Lamb of G-d, as L-RD and Savior! (See 1 Corinthians 6:19-20).

And as an added sign to G-d that I trust in His protection over our lives, I have anointed myself and my husband Jeff with oil as well. I want my heavenly Father to know that I love Him and believe He is still in control. He is our *ADONAI* Rapha (healer) and He alone can guard us from disease.

Today, will you consider anointing yourself and your home in the name of the L-RD? If the Coronavirus ever finds its way into your neighborhood, I am confident the Angel of Death will *pass over* your house because of your visible faith in G-d and who He represents in your life—the L-RD of all.

There's a parallel between what the Israelites did to their homes, and what Yeshua did on the cross for us. The Israelites painted blood on the doorframe, one stroke to the right, and one going the other direction, intersecting in the process. It had to have looked like a cross. It saved their firstborn from certain death.

Through the innocent blood of the Lamb of G-d shed on the cross, we're all saved from eternal separation from *ADONAI* if we believe in this once-and-for-all sin offering. So now, if we ever lie, covet, or dishonor a parent—all violations of the Ten Commandments—we are worthy of death; but G-d passes over us because of the blood of Yeshua painted on our hearts. It's a beautiful comparison, and it makes me so thankful for that sacrifice made for me and all of mankind.

I suspect as *ADONAI* pulls me into a deeper understanding of His Festivals/Feasts, all of the high Holy Days will eventually carry the same reverence and meaning that surrounds Pesach. This observance just seems more personal.

Chapter 6
The Sightings

ADONAI is a personal G-d and desires to have an intimate relationship with His people, but it sometimes takes multiple messages before we hear what He has to say to us. Have you ever experienced a lot of repeat communications from our holy Maker before you finally got it? Or maybe those messages keep presenting themselves, but you're still not seeing what your heavenly Father is trying to tell you. This happened numerous times in Scripture, and often the messenger would appear in bodily form as the Angel of the L-RD. I call these appearances "sightings."

Someone who never got it, even though he had numerous sightings, is the false prophet Balaam, who appears in chapters 22 through 24 in the book of Numbers. Balaam was like The Joker in Batman movies. He was Dick Dastardly from Scooby Doo cartoons. Going further back, you could compare him to Hannibal Lector from *The Silence of the Lambs*.

He was a villain and in my opinion was second in biblical bad-guy status only to Haman from the book of Esther. Around 460 BC, Haman, a royal official under King Xerxes of Persia, tried to eliminate the Jews through a devilish plot, but they were saved by the Jewish-born Queen Esther and her bold intervention. To this day, many Jews remember Haman with "boos and hisses" during the celebration of Purim.

But why is Balaam considered such a scoundrel? Because he was on a mission to curse and destroy the Israelites, at the request of the King of Moab.

As G-d's chosen ones made their way through the wilderness, they camped at Moab's doorstep, and fear began to consume the king of Moab, Balak. The Israelites had already conquered the Amorites as well as the king of Bashon, and Balak was very concerned his people were next. That gripping angst extended to the people of Moab. In Numbers 22:4 (NIV), the Moabites said, "This horde is going to lick up everything around us, as an ox licks up the grass of the field." They thought they were goners; so in his panic, King Balak hired a well-known soothsayer and enemy of the Israelites, Balaam, to curse G-d's people.

Balaam may have originally been from Assyria. If so, he was probably a pagan priest making a living by interpreting dreams, casting spells, and using trickery to predict the future. He may have had a reputation for evil and was a worshiper of many gods, and that list of gods probably included Israel's G-d. My guess is that he was the best at what he did; otherwise, a king would not have sought him out.

So when King Balak's messengers went after Balaam, they arrived with wads of money for his services. They were ready to pay on the spot, but Balaam did something surprising. He wanted to make sure the G-d of the Israelites was in favor of this cursing before he agreed. So he told Balak's crew he wanted to sleep on it and find out if G-d was "all systems go" for the mission to curse Israel.

ADONAI was faithful, even though Balaam was not always faithful to Him. He responded to the sorcerer saying, "Do not go with them. You must not put a curse on those people, because they are blessed" (Numbers 22:12, NIV).

So Balaam listened, and told the messengers to go on home because the L-RD refused to let him go. At that point, Balaam took a step out of his world and into G-d's world. He refused a nice pay day to listen to the greatest G-d in the stockpile of gods he worshipped.

But the persistent king of Moab wasn't going to give up that easily. When he received the news that Balaam had refused to curse the Israelites, he sent other princes from his land, more numerous and more distinguished than the first group he commissioned. They offered Balaam a raise and played to his ego, saying they would do whatever he said, if he would just put a curse on the Israelites.

King Balak was persistent, but Balaam was consistent, and you have to love his faith here. He said, "Even if Balak gave me all the silver and gold in

69

his palace, I could not do anything great or small to go beyond the command of the LORD my God" (Numbers 22:18, NIV) But just in case, Balaam had them stay the night again to make sure G-d hadn't changed his mind.

Know what? G-d did change his mind, kind of. He didn't approve the cursing; but this time, He told Balaam to travel with the group from Moab, but to say and do only what He commanded him to say and do.

Balaam packed his bags, saddled his donkey, and was heading on down the road when the Angel of the L-RD, with a drawn sword in his hand, suddenly blocked the road in an attempt to stop him. Balaam missed the holy roadblock, but the donkey didn't. She got spooked, turned off the road, and hightailed it into a field. Balaam beat his donkey to get her back on the road.

Then the Angel of the L-RD reappeared. This time he stood in a narrow path between two vineyards, with walls on both sides. No field to go to there. The donkey was penned in, and when she saw the Angel of the L-RD this go-around, she pressed close to the wall, crushing Balaam's foot against it. So Balaam whipped her again and was probably thinking, *When I get into town, I'm going to trade this donkey in for a new model.*

They got back on the path, and the Angel of the L-RD made a curtain call, standing this time in a narrow place where there was no room to turn, not to the right or to the left. What did the donkey do?

She plopped down under Balaam, enraging him so much that he beat her with his staff.

The donkey was up to her donkey ears with this treatment, so her true feelings came out—in words! For those old enough to recall the TV show *Mr. Ed*, this may bring back memories:

"Then *ADONAI* opened the donkey's mouth and she said to Balaam, 'What have I done to you that you have beaten me these three times?' Balaam said to the donkey, 'Because you've made a fool of me! If I had a sword in my hand, I would kill you now!'" (Don't you wonder at this point when Balaam would realize he was having a conversation with a donkey?) "The donkey said to Balaam, 'Am I not your donkey which you have ridden as always to this day? Have I ever been in the habit of doing this to you?' 'No,' he said" (Numbers 22:28-30).

Maybe Balaam was finally thinking at this point, *I can't believe I am talking to a donkey!* Then after Balaam's conversation with the beast of burden, the L-RD opened his eyes and he witnessed what the donkey had been seeing all along—the Angel of the L-RD, standing firm in the road with his sword drawn. Whoops! Balaam had run through three stop signs, and now there were flashing lights in front of him. At that point, Balaam bowed low and fell facedown.

So we have to stop and ask here, "Why would G-d do that? Why would He tell Balaam to go, then allow so much trouble on the road?"

The answer: Balaam's heart was divided.

The MacArthur Bible Commentary gives us some insight, saying, "Even though G-d had given Balaam permission to go, He knew that his motive was not right. Thus, the anger of the LORD burned against Balaam because G-d knew that he was not yet submissive to what He required. The result of G-d's confrontation with Balaam was a reaffirmation of the word given in verse 20, repeated in verse 35, that he was to speak only the words that G-d wanted him to speak."[xviii]

G-d also didn't want Balaam to ever look back. We now find him face down before the Angel of the L-RD after the Angel had tried numerous times to get his attention. The fact that his donkey spoke to him pales in comparison to what is before him. At that point, the Angel of the L-RD asks Balaam, "Why have you beaten your donkey these three times? Behold, I came as an adversary because your way before Me is a reckless one! The donkey saw Me and turned away from Me these three times. If she had not turned away from Me, by now I would have killed you indeed, but let her live!' Balaam said to the angel of *ADONAI*, 'I have sinned, for I did not know that you were standing in the road to oppose me. Now, if this is displeasing in your eyes, I will go back home" (Numbers 22:32-34).

But G-d did not undo His agreement to allow Balaam to go to Moab. He reinforced the original decision, commanding Balaam to go with the men, but to only utter the words He would give him. G-d was just making sure there would be no waffling on the assignment.

King Balak was less than enthused with Balaam when he opened his mouth to curse Israel but all that came out were blessings.

"How can I curse those whom God has not cursed? How can I denounce those whom the LORD has not denounced? From the rocky peaks I see them, from the heights I view them. I see a people who live apart and do not consider themselves one of the nations. Who can count the dust of Jacob or number even a fourth of Israel? Let me die the death of the righteous, and may my final end be like theirs!" (Numbers 23:8-10, NIV).

After blessing the Israelites numerous times, Balaam unleashes four more oracles from G-d, one of which is prophetic about the coming Messiah:

"I see Him, but not now; I behold Him, but not near. A star will come out of Jacob; a scepter will rise out of Israel. He will crush the foreheads of Moab, the skulls of all the people of Sheth. Edom will be conquered; Seir, his enemy, will be conquered, but Israel will grow strong. A ruler will come out of Jacob and destroy the survivors of the city" (Numbers 24:17-19, NIV).

You see, this little incident was part of a much bigger picture. The Israelites were G-d's chosen ones; and out of the tribe of Judah, the Messiah, Yeshua HaMashiach, would eventually arrive to save the world, to redeem you and me. G-d's people could not be cursed. They would be protected and no "shaking-in-his-boots" king could prevent the Israelites from claiming the land that was rightfully theirs.

But what troubles me in the story of Balaam is how he could come into contact with the Angel of the L-RD three times on the road to Moab but still plan to betray the Israelites? In fact, he was later part of a plot to entice Israelite men to indulge in sexual immorality with Moabite women. Then, as if it couldn't get worse, those women invited them to be a part of the sacrifices to their false gods.

Because of his role in the betrayal, Balaam was later killed by the Israelites and remembered with disdain throughout Scripture, including the New Testament. When talking about false teachers and the unrighteous, the apostle Peter compares them to Balaam. "They have left the straight way and wandered off to follow the way of Balaam son of Bezer, who loved the wages of wickedness. But he was rebuked for his wrongdoing by a donkey—an animal without speech—who spoke with a human voice and restrained the prophet's madness" (2 Peter 2:15-16, NIV).

Many believe the Angel of the L-RD that Balaam encountered was a pre-incarnate Christ, known as Christophany; yet Balaam still turned away from this supernatural sighting of Yeshua, one of many throughout the Old Testament.

According to Glen Scrivener, author of *3 2 1: The Story of God, the World and You,* "The flood and the ark, the Passover and the Red Sea, the wilderness and the Promised Land, exile and return, war and peace, kingdom and kings, prophets and priests, the Temple, its sacrifices, and its rituals, wisdom in death and in life, songs of lament and rejoicing, the lives of faithful sufferers and the blood of righteous martyrs—the Old Testament is extraordinarily Jesus-shaped."xix

New Testament authors point back to Yeshua in the ancient Scriptures. Scrivener provides five examples:

The "I Am" in whom Abraham rejoiced was Jesus (John 8:56–58).

The L-RD who motivated Moses was Christ (Hebrews 11:26).

The Redeemer who brought them out of Egypt was Jesus (Jude 5).

The Rock in the wilderness was Christ (1 Corinthians 10:4)

The King of Isaiah's Temple vision was the Son (John 12:40–41).xx

However, the Angel of the L-RD's first appearance is found in the book of Genesis when Hagar, Abraham's concubine who is pregnant with his son, Ishmael, is on the run after harsh treatment from Abraham's wife, Sarai. The Angel of the L-RD found Hagar near a spring in the desert and asked, "'Hagar, Sarai's slave-girl, where have you come from and where are you going?' She said, 'I am fleeing from the presence of my mistress Sarai.' The angel of *ADONAI* said, 'Return to your mistress and humble yourself under her hand.' Then the angel of *ADONAI* said to her, 'I will bountifully multiply your seed, and they will be too many to count'" (Genesis 16:7-10).

After that experience, Hagar gave G-d (or Yeshua) the name "El Roi." Translated, it means "the G-d who sees me."

It's interesting that the Angel of the L-RD appeared to Hagar before he appeared to Abraham, who had two sightings. The first was by the oaks of Mamre, when he received three visitors from heaven. During that visit, the Angel of the L-RD announced that Sarah would have a baby at the same time the following year. But this holy trio also announced the impending doom of Sodom and Gomorrah, wiped out because of exceedingly sinful behavior.

The other appearance of the Angel of the L-RD in Abraham's life occurred when he was about to sacrifice the child of the promise, Isaac, because of G-d's command to do so. "Then Abraham reached out his hand and took the knife to slaughter his son. But the Angel of *ADONAI* called to him from heaven and said, 'Abraham! Abraham!' He said, '*Hineni*!' Then He said, 'Do not reach out your hand against the young man—do nothing to him at all. For now I know that you are one who fears God—you did not withhold your son, your only son, from Me'" (Genesis 22:10–12).

In the thicket, Abraham found another sacrifice, a ram that he offered as a burnt offering to the L-RD. It was a foreshadowing of the perfect sacrifice that would later be provided for the cleansing of sin, G-d's only Son, Yeshua.

The Angel of the L-RD also met up with Abraham's grandson Jacob and with Moses in the form of a burning bush. He traveled in front of and behind the Israelites as they made their escape from Egypt. He appeared to Joshua as the Commander of the army of the L-RD. When Joshua realized who he was, he did a face-plant in reverence and asked him, "'What is my LORD saying to His servant?' Then the commander of *ADONAI*'s army replied to Joshua, 'Take your sandal off of your foot, for the place where you are standing is holy.' And Joshua did so" (Joshua 5:14–15).

The Angel of the L-RD reached out to Gideon to give him some holy encouragement as he was commissioned to press into his warrior status and conquer the Midianites. When Gideon realized the Angel of the L-RD was before him, he exclaimed, "Alas, my LORD *ADONAI*! For I have seen the angel of *ADONAI* face to face!" (Judges 6:22).

The Angel of L-RD also encountered Samuel, David, and the Prophet Zechariah. But why would the Angel of the L-RD be Yeshua rather than G-d Himself? You have to look at the meaning of the word "angel." In both the Hebrew and the Greek it means "messenger." So if this was a messenger of G-d or YHWH, it could not be *ADONAI* Himself, but someone who represented *ADONAI*. He had to be pretty high up in heavenly status, because He seemed to have similar knowledge and G-d-like power.

BibleProject draws some conclusions about the Angel of the L-RD that point to this divine visitor as Yeshua Himself. According to their research:

1. **This figure helps us make sense of Jesus' claims.** It seems strange that Jesus would claim he was 'one with the Father' and yet distinct as 'the Son'" (John 10:30). Yet these claims that sound confusing to modern readers fit in the same category as the portrait of the Angel of the L-RD.

2. **This figure creates shelf space for understanding the Trinity.** This ancient and creative way of portraying Yahweh as a complex unity helps readers understand that Yahweh is a diverse yet unified community of love. This is foundational for understanding that perfect community of love—Father, Son, and Spirit—that we have come to call the Trinity.

3. **This figure helps us know G-d's character more.** YHWH interacts on a personal level with humans while also maintaining his identity as G-d above all and entirely other. This G-d takes on an embodied form to relate with humanity, ultimately taking on human flesh to restore humanity to right relationship as partners with him. This complex portrait of the Angel of the L-RD uniquely communicates truths about the character and identity of Yahweh—that he is a complex unity, one who is both unified and diverse, near and above all. What we see in the Angel of the L-RD is brought to a culmination in the person of Jesus, who draws near to humanity in order to draw us near to G-d. [xxi]

Dr. Greg Stone confirms this research by adding, "In Exodus 23, G-d said that the Angel of the L-RD has the power to forgive sin and shares G-d's name. Yet, that angel is a distinct person *from* the person of G-d.

I believe Yeshua was indeed the Angel of the L-RD and was with G-d from the beginning of time. In Genesis 1:26, G-d said, "Let *us* make man in our image, in our likeness…" G-d was clearly not alone at creation. John 1:1–5, says, "In the beginning was the Word. The Word was with God, and the Word was God. He was with God in the beginning. All things were made through Him, and apart from Him nothing was made that has come into being. In Him was life, and the life was the light of men. The light shines in the darkness, and the darkness has not overpowered it." In John 8:12, Yeshua identifies Himself as the light when He says, "I am the light of the world. The one who follows Me will no longer walk in darkness, but will have the light of life."

Before He went to the cross, Yeshua prayed to the Father and said, "I glorified You on earth by finishing the work that You have given Me to do. Now, Father, glorify Me together with Yourself, with the glory which I had with You before the world came to be" (John 17:4–5). And in Revelation 21:6, Yeshua describes Himself as the "Alpha and the Omega, the Beginning and the End."

Appearing as part of the Trinity, Yeshua is an extension of G-d Himself, and revealed additional aspects of His character as He delivered important

news and encouragement and reinforced the plan
that was set from the beginning of time.

Chapter 7
The Prophecy

"How do you know if someone is a prophet? When their prophecies come true." I remember a professor saying these words years ago when we were studying about the numerous prophets in the Bible. Ever since then, when I receive a prophetic word from someone, I hold it close to my heart; but I know if it is true, it will actually come to pass, just as the prophetic message came to pass on my trip to Israel.

Years ago, I received a word about my youngest son, who has wandered away from the faith. I was at an event where a woman began receiving a download from *ADONAI* just for me. She told me to record what she said. As it turned out, the recording did not work. What I remember is that she prophesied about me personally, then about my ministry; but when she began to speak about my son, I *really* paid attention. She said my youngest would have a "Damascus Road" experience that would turn his life around and that I was not to worry about him. The Damascus

Road is where a devout Jew, Saul (later renamed Paul), experienced an encounter with Yeshua. Saul had been breathing murderous threats against followers of Yeshua and was throwing many in jail and approving their executions. The intense light at this Damascus Road meeting was so bright that Saul was temporarily blinded. When his sight was restored, so was his spiritual vision. He was never the same after that. The apostle Paul knew the Torah backward and forward and was educated by the finest teachers, but he had this to say after his life forever changed:

> For it is we who are the circumcision, who worship by the *Ruach Elohim* and glory in Messiah *Yeshua* and have not depended on the flesh—though I myself might have confidence in the flesh also. If anyone else thinks he might depend on the flesh, I far more—circumcised the eighth day; of the nation of Israel; from the tribe of Benjamin; a Hebrew of Hebrews; in regard to the *Torah*, a Pharisee; as for zeal, persecuting Messiah's community; as for *Torah* righteousness, found blameless. But whatever things were gain to me, these I have considered as loss for the sake of the Messiah. More than that, I consider all things to be loss in comparison to the surpassing value of the knowledge of Messiah *Yeshua* my L-RD. Because of Him I have suffered the loss of all things; and I consider them garbage in order that I might gain Messiah and be found in Him not having my righteousness derived from Torah, but one that is through trusting in Messiah—the righteousness from G-d based on trust. My aim is to know Him and the power of His resurrection and the sharing of His

sufferings, becoming like Him in His death— if somehow I might arrive at the resurrection from among the dead" (Philippians 3:3–11).

To date, my son's Damascus Road experience has not occurred, as far as I know; but I have stored this prophetic word in the back of my mind, because if it happens, I will know this person was authentic and a true prophet.

We often scoff when people share a prophecy with us. In our hearts we either don't believe it or don't want to accept it. A biblical example of this can be found in both 1 Kings 22 and 2 Chronicles 18:9–27. King Ahab of Israel and King Jehoshaphat of Judah decided to join forces to fight for a piece of land called Ramoth-gilead that had been stolen by the king of Aram. Before agreeing to move forward, the king of Judah wanted to find out if ADONAI approved of this plan. So Ahab summoned 400 false prophets to tell him what he wanted to hear and they all replied, "Go up, for my L-RD will deliver it into the hand of the king."

The shrewd and godly Jehoshaphat was discerning and asked, "Is there no longer a prophet of *ADONAI* here that we may inquire of Him?"

That wasn't what King Ahab wanted to hear because the prophet of *ADONAI,* Micaiah, refused to play the game and spoke truth, so much so that King Ahab had nothing good to say about him. He complained to Jehoshaphat, "Yes, there is still one by whom we may inquire of *ADONAI*—Micaiah son of Imlah—but I hate him, because he never prophesies good concerning me, only evil" (I Kings 22:8).

Jehoshaphat rebuked Ahab and asked to hear what Micaiah had to say, so Ahab sent a messenger to fetch him.

When the messenger found Micaiah, he tried to influence him to be like the other prophets—to follow the crowd. "'Behold now, the words of the prophets are uniformly declaring favor to the king. So please let your word be like the word of one of them, and speak favorably.' But Micaiah said, 'As *ADONAI* lives, what *ADONAI* says to me, that will I speak'" (Verses 13-14). I saw a plaque once that read, "Speak the truth—even if your voice shakes." I subscribe to that philosophy, but I'll add one additional phrase. "Speak the truth—even if your voice shakes—but do it laced with kindness."

When Micaiah arrived before King Ahab and King Jehoshaphat, the king of Israel asked, "Micaiah, should we march to Ramoth-gilead in battle or should we refrain?" After a sarcastic response, Micaiah went counter-cultural on King Ahab and said, "I saw all Israel scattered on the hills, as sheep without a shepherd. Then *ADONAI* said, 'These have no master; let each of them return home in peace'" (Verses 15-17).

King Ahab was not happy with this response. "And the king of Israel said to Jehoshaphat, 'Didn't I tell you that he wouldn't prophesy good concerning me, only evil?'"

Micaiah delivered more bad news for Ahab, "Therefore hear the word of *ADONAI*. I saw *ADONAI* sitting on His throne, with all the hosts of heaven standing by Him on His right hand and on

His left. Then *ADONAI* said, 'Who will entice Ahab to go up and fall at Ramoth-gilead?' One suggested this and another that, until a certain spirit came forward and stood before *ADONAI* and said, 'I will entice him.' So *ADONAI* asked him, 'How?' And he said: 'I will go and be a deceiving spirit in the mouth of all his prophets.' Then He said: 'You shall entice him and shall prevail also—go and do so.' Now therefore, behold, *ADONAI* has put a deceiving spirit in the mouth of all these prophets of yours, and *ADONAI* has decreed evil upon you" (1 Kings 22:18–23).

After that, one of King Ahab's false prophets, Zedekiah, slapped Micaiah in the face, and Ahab had Micaiah arrested. Before being taken away, Micaiah got in one last word: "If you ever return safely, then *ADONAI* has not spoken through me" (Verse 28). Then he added, and I'll paraphrase, "Did you get that, people?"

So was Micaiah a true prophet or a false prophet?

Both King Ahab and King Jehoshaphat disregarded Micaiah's warning, and went into battle against the king of Aram and his men. The Arameans' target was the king of Israel, Ahab, who declared war on them; but he was difficult to pinpoint because he disguised himself in this battle. However, an Aramean soldier randomly shot at the Israelite troops and somehow, like a guided missile, that arrow landed between the joints of King Ahab's armor, mortally wounding him. By evening, he had died. So the moral of the story is, I guess the two kings should have listened to Micaiah. He was a true prophet.

In the same way, G-d gave advance notice about His Son, Yeshua, throughout Scripture; and it did become reality, providing a stamp of authenticity for those prophets who were given the advance details about Yeshua and His life, death, and resurrection.

In an article by Sheri Bell for Josh McDowell Ministries, she said there are over 300 predictions of Jesus's arrival in the Old Testament. Apologist Peter Stoner says the odds of any man fulfilling even 48 of those prophesies jumps to 10 to the 157th power.[xxii] That stat should be enough to keep you reading about what's to come.

One of the places where you can find prophetic words about Yeshua is in the book of Psalms, or the "Sefer Tehillim," as it's known in Jewish liturgy. One of the most famous is Psalm 22, written by King David, king of Israel from 1109-969 BC.[xxiii]

King David, who followed Saul as King, starts off Psalm 22 with the words "My God, my God, why have you forsaken me?" (Psalm 22:2). These were Yeshua's exact words found in Matthew 27:46: *Eli, Eli, lema sabachthani?* Later in Psalm 22, it appears David is prophesying about Yeshua's perspective from the cross when He says: "Am I a worm, and not a man? Am I a scorn of men, despised by people? All who see me mock me. They curl their lips, shaking their heads: 'Rely on *ADONAI*! Let Him deliver him! Let Him rescue him— since He delights in Him!'" (Psalm 22:7–9).

Earlier in Matthew 27, we see the similar abuse that Yeshua endured, "They stripped Him and put a scarlet robe on Him, and then twisted together a crown of thorns and set it on His head. They put a staff in His right hand. Then they knelt in front of Him and mocked Him. 'Hail, king of the Jews!' they said. They spit on Him, and took the staff and struck Him on the head again and again. After they had mocked Him, they took off the robe and put His own clothes on Him. Then they led Him away to crucify Him" (Verses 28-31, NIV). However, it is in Matthew 27:41–43 that you see the almost exact words David penned: "Likewise the ruling *kohanim*, along with the *Torah* scholars and elders, were also mocking Him. 'He saved others,' they were saying, 'but He can't save Himself? He's the King of Israel! Let Him come down now from the stake, and we'll believe in Him! He trusts in God; let God rescue Him now, if He wants Him. For He said, 'I am *Ben-Elohim.*'"

The most compelling parallel between Psalm 22 and Yeshua's experience is found in the passage that stretches from Psalm 22:15-19: "I am poured out like water, and all my bones are disjointed. My heart is like wax—melting within my innards. My strength is dried up like a clay pot, my tongue clings to my jaws. You lay me in the dust of death. For dogs have surrounded me. A band of evildoers has closed in on me. They pierced my hands and my feet. I can count all my bones. They stare, they gape at me. They divide my clothes among them, and cast lots for my garment."

In John 19:28 it parallels the previous passage about Yeshua's thirst: "After this, when *Yeshua* knew that all things were now completed, to fulfill the Scripture He said, 'I am thirsty.'"

The words from Psalm 22 were written by King David 1,000 years before the time of Christ. He could not have known what was going to happen to Yeshua except through receiving a prophetic word.

Yeshua was crucified. He was condemned to death by the Roman Governor over Judea, Pontius Pilate, who reigned from 26-37 AD. Pilate saw Yeshua as an innocent individual and wanted to release him, but Scripture said he gave in to the cries of the people who shouted, "Crucify Him! Crucify Him!" Pilate ended up releasing a man who had been thrown into prison for insurrection and murder and gave the order to put Yeshua to death. After He was scourged, (beaten with a short whip consisting of several heavy, leather thongs, with two small balls of lead attached near the ends of each) He was crucified on a cross. Here were the latter stages of crucifixion as explained by Dr. C. Truman Davis in an article titled, "A Physician's View of the Crucifixion of Jesus Christ."

> "Jesus experienced hours of limitless pain, cycles of twisting, joint-rending cramps, intermittent partial asphyxiation, searing pain where tissue is torn from His lacerated back as He moves up and down against the rough timber. Then another agony begins -- a terrible crushing pain deep in the chest as the pericardium slowly fills with serum and begins to compress the heart. One remembers again the 22nd

Psalm, the 14th verse: 'I am poured out like water, and all my bones are out of joint; my heart is like wax; it is melted in the midst of my bowels.'

It is now almost over. The loss of tissue fluids has reached a critical level; the compressed heart is struggling to pump heavy, thick, sluggish blood into the tissue; the tortured lungs are making a frantic effort to gasp in small gulps of air. The markedly dehydrated tissues send their flood of stimuli to the brain. Jesus gasps His fifth cry, 'I thirst.' One remembers another verse from the prophetic 22nd Psalm: 'My strength is dried up like a potsherd; and my tongue cleaveth to my jaws; and thou has brought me into the dust of death.' A sponge soaked in posca, the cheap, sour wine which is the staple drink of the Roman legionaries, is lifted to His lips. He apparently doesn't take any of the liquid.

The body of Jesus is now in extremes, and He can feel the chill of death creeping through His tissues. This realization brings out His sixth words, possibly little more than a tortured whisper, 'It is finished.' His mission of atonement has completed. Finally He can allow His body to die. With one last surge of strength, He once again presses His torn feet against the nail, straightens His legs, takes a deeper breath, and utters His seventh and last cry, 'Father! Into thy hands I commit my spirit.'"[xxiv]

There were numerous witnesses of Yeshua's crucifixion that day, over 2,000 years ago. The apostles wrote about it in the New Testament; and during the time of persecution that followed, most of them were martyred because they could not deny what they experienced, before and after the resurrection of Yeshua. According to Christian tradition, the Apostle Peter refused to be crucified right side up, like his Rabbi Jesus was crucified. Instead he was placed on a cross with his head down, because he did not feel worthy to die the same type of death that Yeshua died.[xxv]

The crucifixion of Yeshua was also recorded by a reputable Jewish historian of the day named Josephus, in the book *Jewish Antiquities*.

> About this time there lived Jesus, a wise man, if indeed one ought to call Him a man. For he was one who performed surprising deeds and was a teacher of such people as accept the truth gladly. He won over many Jews and many of the Greeks. He was the Messiah. And when, upon the accusation of the principal men among us, Pilate had condemned Him to a cross, those who had first come to love Him did not cease. He appeared to them spending a third day restored to life, for the prophets of G-d had foretold these things and a thousand other marvels about Him. And the tribe of the Christians, so called after Him, has still to this day not disappeared.[xxvi]

Completing our analysis of the prophetic words found in Psalm 22, we examine this verse: "They divide my clothes among them and cast lots for my garment." There is no record of this ever happening to King David. Toward the end of his life, David's body grew cold and was warmed by concubines (1 Kings 1:2). After watching his son, Solomon, take over the throne,

1 Kings 2:10 (NIV) says, "Then David rested with his ancestors and was buried in the City of

David." The prophetic word in Psalm 22 was about Yeshua through David, not about the king's journey. In Matthew 27:35 (NIV), it clearly confirms this prophesy about Yeshua's death when it says, "When they had crucified Him, they divided up His clothes by casting lots."

However, my favorite prophetic writing that points to Yeshua's life and purpose is found in the book of Isaiah. In Judaism, Isaiah is considered a "latter prophet." In Jewish literature, the book of Isaiah is included with other prophetic books like Jeremiah, Ezekiel, and twelve minor prophets including Obadiah, Hosea and Zechariah.[xxvii]

Isaiah was not only a prophet called by G-d; he also stood in the presence of YHWH, and through his experience gives us an image of how the throne of G-d appears:

In the year of King Uzziah's death, I saw *ADONAI* sitting on a throne, high and lifted up, and the train of His robe filled the Temple. Seraphim were standing above Him. Each had six wings: with two he covered his face and with two he covered his feet, and with two he flew. One called out to another, and said: "Holy, holy, holy, is *ADONAI*-Tzva'ot! The whole earth is full of His glory." Then the posts of the door trembled at the voice of those who called, and the House was filled with smoke. Then I said: "Oy to me! For I am ruined! For I am a man of unclean lips, and I am dwelling among a people of unclean lips. For my eyes have seen the King, *ADONAI*-Tzva'ot!" Then one of the seraphim flew to me, with a glowing coal in his hand, which he had taken with tongs from the altar. He touched my mouth with it and said:

91

"Behold, this has touched your lips. Your iniquity is taken away, and your sins atoned for." Then I heard the voice of *ADONAI* saying: "Whom should I send, and who will go for Us?" So I said, "*Hineni.* Send me" (Isaiah 6:1–8).

According to an article by Jacob Isaacs, author of *Our People: A History of the Jews*, "Isaiah's mission was not only to admonish the people to keep them on the right path. He also instilled fervent faith in G-d in the hearts of his flock, and he brought them courage and fortitude at a time when they were suffering mortal fear from the threat of the new Assyrian Empire. Isaiah also described in glowing terms the future glory of Zion, which inspires our people to the present day."[xxviii]

Isaiah also gave detailed information about the coming Messiah in Isaiah 53. This chapter has been a stumbling block for many Jews, and for the most part has been eliminated from readings in the synagogue. According to Dr. Eitan Bar in an article, "Isaiah 53—The Forbidden Chapter," "The 17th century Jewish historian, Raphael Levi, admitted that long ago the rabbis used to read Isaiah 53 in synagogues, but after the chapter caused 'arguments and great confusion' the rabbis decided that the simplest thing would be to just take that prophecy out of the Haftarah readings in synagogues. That's why today when we read Isaiah 52, we stop in the middle of the chapter and the week after we jump straight to Isaiah 54."[xxix]

So what verbiage in Isaiah 53 caused so much controversy? Why would a part of the historic Word of G-d be skipped over in liturgy read at services?

It is because the parallel and prophetic words concerning the coming Messiah are too close to the circumstances that surrounded the life, death, and resurrection of Yeshua.

We'll look at Isaiah 53 in its entirety, then draw some parallels.

Isaiah 53

Who has believed our report? To whom is the arm of *ADONAI* revealed? [2] For He grew up before Him like a tender shoot, like a root out of dry ground. He had no form or majesty that we should look at Him, nor beauty that we should desire Him. [3] He was despised and rejected by men, a man of sorrows, acquainted with grief, One from whom people hide their faces. He was despised, and we did not esteem Him. [4] Surely He has borne our griefs and carried our pains. Yet we esteemed Him stricken, struck by God, and afflicted. [5] But He was pierced because of our transgressions, crushed because of our iniquities. The chastisement for our shalom was upon Him, and by His stripes we are healed. [6] We all like sheep have gone astray. Each of us turned to his own way. So *ADONAI* has laid on Him the iniquity of us all. [7] He was oppressed and He was afflicted yet He did not open His mouth. Like a lamb led to the slaughter, like a sheep before its shearers is silent, so He did not open His mouth. [8] Because of oppression and judgment He was taken away. As for His generation, who considered? For He was cut off from the land of the living, for the transgression of my people—the stroke was theirs. [9] His grave was given with the wicked, and by a rich man in His death, though He had done no violence, nor was there any deceit in His mouth. [10] Yet it pleased *ADONAI* to bruise Him. He caused Him to suffer. If He makes His soul a guilt offering, He will see His offspring, He will prolong His days, and the will of *ADONAI* will succeed by His hand. [11] As a result of the anguish of His soul He will see it and be satisfied by His knowledge. The Righteous One, My Servant will make many righteous and He will bear their iniquities. [12] Therefore I will give Him a portion with the great, and He will divide the spoil with the mighty—because He poured out His soul to death, and was counted with transgressors. For He bore the sin of many, and interceded for the transgressors (Isaiah 53:1–12).

Now let's take this verse by verse and see the parallels from Isaiah 53 to the life of Yeshua.

Verse 2: "For He grew up before Him like a tender shoot, like a root out of dry ground." Isaiah 11:1 speaks about this shoot as well: "A shoot will spring up from the stump of Jesse, and a branch from his roots will bear fruit." Isaiah 4:2 also provides an agricultural analogy: "On that day the Branch of the L-RD will be beautiful and glorious, and the fruit of the land will be the pride and glory of Israel's survivors."

In Matthew 1, Yeshua's genealogy is provided. His lineage originated in the Tribe of Judah which means Jesse, the father of King David, is a member of his family tree. Yeshua is a shoot that sprung up from the "stump of Jesse." Meanwhile, in John 15:5

(NIV), Yeshua provides an image of Himself as a vine when He says, "I am the vine; you are the branches. If you remain in me and I in you, you will bear much fruit; apart from me you can do nothing."

Verse 3: He was despised and rejected by men, a man of sorrows, acquainted with grief, One from whom people hide their faces. Throughout His public ministry, Yeshua experienced both great love and great disdain. Yeshua and His disciples were Jewish and many of the early believers were also Jewish. It was the Jewish leaders of the day, the Pharisees and Sanhedrin, who consistently criticized Yeshua and tried to regularly entrap Him. Early in Yeshua's ministry, the teachers of the law came down from Jerusalem to where Yeshua was preaching and healing people and deduced, "He's possessed by beelzebul," and, "By the ruler of demons He drives out demons" (Mark 3:22).

In Mark 7, the Pharisees and the teachers of the law witnessed Yeshua and some of His disciples eating food before washing their hands. That drew criticism and a sharp response from the attackers. Let's listen in on the conversation:

"'Why don't Your disciples walk according to the tradition of the elders? Why do they eat bread with unwashed hands?' And He said to them, 'Rightly did Isaiah prophesy about you hypocrites, as it is written, 'This people honors Me with their lips but their heart is far from Me. And in vain they worship Me, teaching as doctrines the commandments of men. Having left behind the commandment of God, you hold on to the tradition of men.'"

Later, using this exercise with the accusers as a teaching example, Yeshua told the crowd,

"Hear Me, everyone, and understand. There is nothing outside the man that can make him unholy by going into him. Rather, it is what comes out of the man that makes the man unholy" (Mark 7:14–15).

The religious leaders also questioned Yeshua's authority and they tried to trip Him up on Scriptural knowledge. One of the teachers of the law asked Yeshua to name the most important commandment. Yeshua responded, "'You shall love *ADONAI* your God with all your heart, and with all your soul, and with all your mind.' This is the first and greatest commandment. And the second is like it, 'You shall love your neighbor as yourself.' The entire Torah and the Prophets hang on these two commandments'" (Matthew 22:37–40).

It was after this response, Scripture says, that no one dared to ask Yeshua any more questions. Instead, the religious leaders began to plot His arrest and plan His ultimate death by crucifixion.

Yeshua was also rejected by residents of His home town. When He went into the Nazareth synagogue to teach, people He probably knew growing up ridiculed Him. They asked questions like: "Where did this man get these things?" "What's this wisdom that has been given Him?" "What are these remarkable miracles He is performing?" "Isn't this the carpenter, Mary's son and the brother of James, Joseph, Judas and Simon?" "Aren't his sisters here with us?" (Mark 6:2-3). I wonder sometimes if people I grew up with say the same things about me.

"Wasn't she the gawky girl with glasses?" "She wore the same things over and over, right?" "I don't remember her ever doing anything spectacular in high school." "Who does she think she is?"

The despised and rejected Yeshua responded by saying, "A prophet is not without honor except in his own town, among his relatives and in his own home" (Verse 4). Because of their unbelief, Yeshua was unable to do miracles there, except to heal a few who were sick.

Verses 4–5: "Surely He has borne our griefs and carried our pains. Yet we esteemed Him stricken, struck by God, and afflicted. But He was pierced because of our transgressions, crushed because of our iniquities. The chastisement for our shalom was upon Him, and by His stripes we are healed."

History supports that Yeshua was crucified. The sticking point has always been evidence for the resurrection, even though the Bible reports there were over 500 at one time who saw Yeshua post-resurrection, and He also appeared to His core group of disciples as well as the women who were close to him, including His mother Mary and Mary Magdalene. Except for John, who spent his last days in exile, His disciples were all martyred for their faith. It's hard to believe that these men would go to their deaths for a lie. Apologist Lee Strobel said in his book, *The Case for Christ*, "People will die for their religious beliefs if they sincerely believe they're true, but people won't die for their religious beliefs if they know their beliefs are false."[xxx]

In a 2017 article by Bob Hostetler and Josh McDowell called "If I Had Faked the Resurrection," the two authors say they would have done things differently if they had fabricated the resurrection. One point is that they would have waited a longer period of time before publishing the account. In the article, they said, "Few historians dispute the fact that the disciples of Jesus began preaching the news of His resurrection soon after the event itself; in fact, Peter's Pentecost sermon (Acts 2) occurred within 50 days of the Resurrection. And textual research indicates that the written accounts of the Resurrection, especially the creedal statement of 1 Corinthians 15:3–8, are astoundingly early in origin, possibly within two years of the event. Such early origins argue against any notion that the Resurrection accounts are legendary."xxxi

The apologists also said they would surround the event with impressive supernatural displays and omens. "As Jewish scholar Pinchas Lapide writes, 'We do not read in the first testimonies [of the Resurrection] of an apocalyptic spectacle, exorbitant sensations, or of the transforming impact of a cosmic event. . . According to all New-Testament reports, no human eye saw the resurrection itself, no human being was present, and none of the disciples asserted to have apprehended, let alone understood, its manner and nature. How easy it would have been for them or their immediate successors to supplement this scandalous hole in the concatenation of events by fanciful embellishments! But precisely because none of the evangelists dared to 'improve upon' or embellish this unseen resurrection, the total picture of the gospels also gains in trustworthiness."ᵡˣˣⁱⁱ

The Bible also reported that women were the first to see the risen Christ. In Matthew 28, it says that Yeshua appeared to Mary Magdalene and His mother, Mary. Scripture says Yeshua's appearance was "like lightening and His clothes were white as snow." If someone were writing a fictional story in a patriarchal society, they never would have allowed two women to be the first to witness the resurrected Yeshua. This account was there because Yeshua was resurrected from the dead and it was truth. It's a resurrection that has provided the inexplicable power for many to overcome sinful lifestyles and unhealthy mindsets, resulting in what the Bible calls "a new creation" (see 2 Corinthians 5:17).

It was actually a "Resurrection service" that led to a complete transformation of Ellen Collins' life. Ellen was born into a Reformed Jewish household. Both her parents are Jewish, and they celebrated the Jewish holidays, recited the Shabbat blessings every Friday evening, and went to synagogue. She also went to "Shul" in preparation for her Bat Mitzvah. Her two favorite Jewish holidays were Chanukah and Purim. However, it was a very difficult season in her life that led her to search for hope. "I was at a very low point in my life where I felt suicidal again," said Ellen. "I tried to commit suicide when I was younger but thankfully was unsuccessful. I felt like there was a huge void in my heart. Nothing or nobody, including my child, could fulfill it. I felt like I didn't know who I was. I was very lost."

So when Ellen's Gentile friend invited her to the Resurrection service at her church, she figured she would give G-d a try as her last straw. She had witnessed the change in her friend, who had given her life to the L-RD. *If G-d can't help*, Ellen thought, *my life is over*. So she decided to go to church.

Ellen picks up the story from there. "That day, Resurrection Sunday/Passover 1995, I gave my life to the L-RD, as I had a supernatural encounter with Him in the service. But right after that I had a problem receiving Yeshua fully into my heart because I was raised in fear of the name of Jesus." However, Ellen had a wonderful beginning getting to know G-d the Father better. She began to identify with Him as her G-d, and she started to see herself as part of Israel and the land as being her Jewish heritage. Ellen said, "My life started to make sense. I did pray to G-d to help my heart receive Yeshua. Not too long after that, I was in a service and as I lifted my hands to worship the L-RD, I had a vision of the hands of Yeshua and His nail scarred hand right in front of me. It was then that I not only saw Yeshua as Messiah, but as my Jewish big brother."

Ellen's life was resurrected after that. Her heart was made whole, as the void was filled when she came into her identity as a child of G-d and who she is as a Jew. She now serves as an associate pastor who oversees Jewish and Christian relations, and she also leads a ministry called One New Man.

Yeshua died on the cross for Ellen. He gave His life for you and also for me. But what are some of the additional prophesies that were fulfilled about

100

Yeshua? We read a doctor's detailed and horrifying description of what occurs when someone is crucified, and in John 19 we see the evidence of Yeshua being "pierced." John writes:

Now it was the day of Preparation, and the next day was to be a special Sabbath. Because the Jewish leaders did not want the bodies left on the crosses during the Sabbath, they asked Pilate to have His legs broken and the bodies taken down. The soldiers therefore came and broke the legs of the first man who had been crucified with Jesus, and then those of the other. But when they came to Jesus and found that He was already dead, they did not break His legs. Instead, one of the soldiers *pierced* Jesus's side with a spear, bringing a sudden flow of blood and water (John 19:31-35 NIV).

When we look at the last part of verse 5 in Isaiah 53, "…and by His wounds we are healed," there are many directions we can travel with that phrase. I believe one thing it's telling us is that because of Yeshua's wounds, our broken relationship with G-d was healed. There had to be a once-and-for-all sacrifice. An unblemished lamb was required to give up His life so the "Angel of Death" would pass over us and we could attain eternal life. Our salvation required a lasting sacrifice. Our sinful selves could never stand in the presence of G-d without it.

I look at my own life as a fatherless girl with a mentally ill mother. There is no reason that I should even be alive today; but, miraculously, my childhood wounds were healed thanks to the sacrifice of Yeshua and the changes that occurred in me after I gave my life completely to Him. My eyes were opened to the fact that although my earthly father died before I was born, I am not fatherless, because in Psalm 68:5, G-d says He is a "Father to the fatherless." We see that message of G-d as Father throughout the New Testament, but it hinges on belief in His Son. John 1:12 says, "But to all who did receive Him, to those who believed in His name, He gave the right to become children of God." This was made possible only through Yeshua's wounds.

In the *Spirit Filled Life Bible,* Executive Editor Jack Hayford says:

Isaiah 53 clearly teaches that bodily healing is included in the atoning work of Christ, His suffering and His cross. The Hebrew words for "griefs" and "sorrows" specifically mean physical affliction. This is verified in the fact that Matthew 8:17 says this Isaiah text is being exemplarily fulfilled in Jesus's healing people of human sickness and other physical need. Further, that the words "borne" and "carried" refer to Jesus's atoning work on the cross is made clear by the fact that they are the same words used to describe Christ's bearing our sins (see v.11; also, 1 Peter 2:24). These texts unequivocally link the grounds of provision for both our salvation and our healing to the atoning work of Calvary. Neither is automatically appropriated, however; for each provision—a soul's eternal salvation or a person's temporal, physical healing—must be received by faith. Christ's work on the cross makes each possible: simple faith receives each as we choose."[xxxiii]

Verse 6: "We all like sheep have gone astray. Each of us turned to his own way. So *ADONAI* has laid on Him the iniquity of us all." The sheep analogy is interesting here, as Yeshua refers to "sheep" in the tenth chapter of John:

I am the Good Shepherd. The Good Shepherd lays down His life for the sheep. The hired worker is not the shepherd, and the sheep are not his own. He sees the wolf coming and abandons the sheep and flees. Then the wolf snatches and scatters the sheep. The man is only a hired hand and does not care about the sheep. I am the Good Shepherd. I know My own and My own know Me, just as the Father knows Me and I know the Father. And I lay down My life for the sheep. I have other sheep that are not from this fold; those also I must lead, and they will listen to My voice. So there shall be one flock, one Shepherd. For this reason the Father loves Me, because I lay down My life, so that I may take it up again" (John 10:11–17).

Then in 1 Peter 2:24–25, the Apostle Peter almost repeats the words of Isaiah verbatim when he says, "He Himself bore our sins in His body on the tree, so that we, removed from sins, might live for righteousness. By His wounds you were healed. For you like sheep were going astray but now you have returned to the Shepherd and Guardian of your souls."

The Apostle Peter saw Yeshua as the fulfillment of Isaiah's prophecy.

Over the years, I have heard the Shepherd's voice; and in the times He speaks, I am certain the words are from Him, because it's almost as if He interrupts my thought so I cannot attribute what I am hearing to "self-talk." I remember attending a board retreat for a media organization I am involved in, Christian Women in Media. I was having a conversation with a friend outside one of the houses on the retreat property. She was telling me that she was a biology and chemistry major in college and those were subjects where she excelled. Even though my father was a doctor, biology was my worst subject in both high school and college. I thought I made a "C" in high school biology because I had a crush on a boy in my class, and that had diverted my focus; but in college there was no crush, and the result was the same. I told her how impressed I was with her success and said, "I was not destined to be a doctor like my dad, because I always struggled with biology."

And that's when I heard, *You may not be a doctor like your father, but I gifted you to heal.*

This friend knew I had received a word, as I stopped talking and stood in silence. It was the Shepherd's voice, and there was no mistaking who was speaking to me. Over the years I have laid hands on many people and have witnessed supernatural healing. I have a heart to see people healed emotionally as well through the ministry *ADONAI* gave me, Pearls of Promise. Healing is my primary calling, and my Shepherd confirmed it when He joined our conversation.

Verses 7–8: "He was oppressed and He was afflicted yet He did not open His mouth. Like a lamb led to the slaughter, like a sheep before its shearers is silent, so He did not open His mouth. Because of oppression and judgment He was taken away."

When Yeshua was on trial and standing before the governor of Judea, Pontius Pilate, He was accused by the chief priests and the elders. Yeshua gave no response to their accusations as they pointed fingers at Him. Pilate asked, "Don't you hear the testimony they are bringing against you?" Again Yeshua "did not open His mouth." Matthew 27:14 says, "*Yeshua* did not answer, not even one word, so the governor was greatly amazed."

I am sure the Lamb of G-d knew His destiny was set; and at this point, nothing He could say would save Him.

And as Isaiah 53:8 prophesies, there was oppression and judgment before Yeshua went to the cross. Matthew 27 goes on to give a snapshot of the Son of G-d's public humiliation.

They stripped Him and put a scarlet robe around Him. And after braiding a crown of thorns, they placed it on His head and put a staff in His right hand. And falling on their knees before Him, they mocked Him, saying, 'Hail, King of the Jews!' They spat on Him, and they took the staff and beat Him over and over on the head. When they finished mocking Him, they stripped the robe off Him and put His own clothes back on Him. And they led Him away to crucify Him (Matthew 27: 28–31).

There is no doubt that "Because of oppression and judgment He was taken away."

Verse 10: "Yet it pleased *ADONAI* to bruise Him. He caused Him to suffer. If He makes His soul a guilt offering, He will see His offspring, He will prolong His days, and the will of *ADONAI* will succeed by His hand."

Prior to the cross, Yeshua, knowing what was ahead, spent time with His *ADONAI* and asked Him to change His mind about His plan to save the world. After being transparent with His disciples and sharing that His soul was "overwhelmed with sorrow to the point of death," Yeshua began to pray to His heavenly Father: "My Father, if it is possible, may this cup be taken from me. Yet not as I will, but as you will" (Matthew 26:38–39, NIV). This statement backs up Isaiah's prophecy that it was G-d's will to crush Yeshua and cause Him to suffer as an offering for our sin. It was *ADONAI's* plan to sacrifice His only Son for the sins of the world.

The section of Isaiah 53:10 that says, "He will see His offspring and prolong His days" can be confusing, because Yeshua did not have any children. However, the reference to "offspring" refers to "spiritual" children; and in this light, Yeshua has countless offspring, more than can be counted. *Barnes Notes on the Bible* adds further explanation:

> The language here is taken from that which was regarded as the highest blessing among the Hebrews. With them length of days and a numerous posterity were regarded as the highest favors, and usually as the clearest proofs of the divine love. "Children's children are the crown of old men" (Proverbs 17:6). [Also see] Psalm 127:5. Psalm 128:6: "Yea, thou shalt see thy

children's children, and peace upon Israel." So one of the highest blessings which could be promised to Abraham was that he would be made the father of many nations. [See] Genesis 12:2, Genesis 17:5–6. In accordance with this, the Messiah is promised that he shall see a numerous spiritual posterity. A similar declaration occurs in Psalm 22:30, which is usually applied to the Messiah. "A seed shall serve Him; it shall be accounted to the L-RD for a generation."[xxxiv]

According to Pew Research, in 2015 there were 2.3 billion Christians in the world, making up 31.2 percent of the world's population, and it is still the largest religious group.[xxxv] Friends, that represents a lot of offspring.

Verse 11: "As a result of the anguish of His soul He will see it and be satisfied by His knowledge. The Righteous One, My Servant will make many righteous **and He will bear their iniquities."**

The Holman Illustrated Bible Commentary sheds some light on this passage. "The Servant's pain, suffering and death will function like a restitution offering (Leviticus 5:14–6:7; 7:1–10)—a sacrifice offered when there was a 'transgression against the sacred things of the L-RD.' The sin of G-d's people was such a transgression."[xxxvi] We were justified through Yeshua's sacrifice.

The Merriam Webster online dictionary defines the word "justify" as: "to judge, regard, or treat as righteous and worthy of salvation."[xxxvii] I heard my pastor once say it is "just-as-if-I'd never sinned."

The apostle Paul talks about this concept of justification:

But now apart from the law the righteousness of G-d has been made known, to which the Law and the Prophets testify. This righteousness is given through faith in Jesus Christ to all who believe. There is no difference between Jew and Gentile, for all have sinned and fall short of the glory of G-d, and all are justified freely by His grace through the redemption that came by Christ Jesus. G-d presented Christ as a sacrifice of atonement, through the shedding of His blood—to be received by faith. He did this to demonstrate His righteousness, because in His forbearance He had left the sins committed beforehand unpunished—He did it to demonstrate His righteousness at the present time, so as to be just and the one who justifies those who have faith in Jesus (Romans 3:21–26, NIV).

For many years, I was blind to my own sin and did not understand the extent of this gift of justification. I held a grudge against my own mother for the emotional abandonment that occurred in my life. For about seventeen years, I did not have anything to do with my mother. But after I rededicated my life to G-d and Yeshua, G-d took the scales off my eyes and opened them up to the grace and justification I'd benefited from in my own life. I had been forgiven for so much. It was at that point, I realized, "Who was I not to forgive my mother?" So I forgave my mother and honored her, as commanded by *ADONAI,* toward the end of her life. It was not until I forgave and honored my mother that I could be used in any form of ministry.

Verse 12: "Therefore I will give Him a portion with the great, and He will divide the spoil with the mighty—because He poured out His soul to death, and was counted with transgressors. For He bore the sin of many, and interceded for the transgressors."

We receive a peek at Yeshua's greatness throughout the New Testament. Prior to his stoning in Acts 7, Stephen, a post-ascension follower of Yeshua and "full of the *Ruach ha-Kodesh*," looked up to heaven and saw G-d's glory and Yeshua nearby. Stephen said, "'Look, I see heavens opened and the Son of Man standing at the right hand of God" (Acts 7:56).

The apostle Paul attempts to paint a picture of Yeshua's greatness to the Ephesian believers in Ephesians 1 when he says:

> I pray that the eyes of your heart may be enlightened, so that you may know what is the hope of His calling, what is the richness of His glorious inheritance in the *kedoshim*, and what is His exceedingly great power toward us who keep trusting Him—in keeping with the working of His mighty strength. This power He exercised in Messiah when He raised Him from the dead and seated Him at His right hand in heaven. He is far above any ruler, authority, power, leader, and every name that is named—not only in the *olam ha-zeh* but also in the *olam ha-ba*. G-d placed all things under Messiah's feet and appointed Him as head over all things for His community—which is His body, the fullness of Him who fills all in all (Ephesians 1:18–23).

But there is no greater image of Yeshua than the one the Apostle John recounts in Revelation 1:

"Then I turned to see the voice that was speaking to me. And when I turned, I saw seven golden *menorot*. In the midst of the *menorot*, I saw One like a Son of Man, clothed in a robe down to His feet, with a golden belt wrapped around His chest. His head and His hair were white like wool, white like snow, and His eyes like a flame of fire. His feet were like polished bronze refined in a furnace, and His voice was like the roar of rushing waters. In His right hand He held seven stars, and out of His mouth came forth a sharp, two-edged sword. His face was like the sun shining at full strength. When I saw Him, I fell at His feet like a dead man. But He placed His right hand on me, saying, 'Do not be afraid! I am the First and the Last, and the One who lives. I was dead, but look—I am alive forever and ever! Moreover, I hold the keys of death and *Sheol*'" (Revelation 1:12–18).

The prophet Daniel also saw a similar image of Yeshua, as described in Daniel 10:5–6: "I lifted my eyes and looked, and behold, a man dressed in linen with a belt of fine gold from Uphaz around his waist. His body was like yellow jasper, his face like a flash of lightning, his eyes like fiery torches, his arms and his feet like the gleam of burnished bronze, and the sound of his words like the roar of a multitude."

Yeshua fulfilled this next aspect of Isaiah 53:12 on the cross: "and was numbered with the transgressors. For He bore the sin of many, and made intercession for the transgressors." As Yeshua hung on the cross, He was not thinking about

110

Himself. He was forgiving those who put Him there. In Luke 23:34, Jesus said, "Father, forgive them, for they do not know what they are doing." His cross was placed between two criminals who hung on either side of Him. One of the criminals mocked Yeshua, but there must have been something supernatural about the "King of the Jews" that reached the other criminal. He saw the glory of G-d in Yeshua's battered and bloody body and said, "*Yeshua*, remember me when You come into Your kingdom." *Yeshua* said to him, "Amen, I tell you, today you shall be with Me in Paradise" (Luke 23:42–43).

Even the circumstances surrounding Yeshua's death and resurrection were very "Jewish." In his book, *The Handbook for the End Times*, author Don Finto explains that Yeshua really wasn't crucified on Good Friday, nor was He raised to life on Easter. Yeshua's death, burial, and resurrection all coincided with the Jewish calendar. According to Finto, "He was executed on Passover and raised on the Festival of First Fruits. His sinless life is symbolized throughout the Festival of Unleavened Bread, and He poured out His Spirit on Pentecost."[xxxviii]

Is this merely coincidence, or did G-d have an intricate plan for His chosen ones that dates back to the Torah? It's difficult to deny the similarities between the prophetic words spoken many centuries prior to Yeshua's birth and the circumstances surrounding Yeshua's life, death, and resurrection.

I had stated earlier that there are at least 300 Messianic prophecies found in the Old Testament.

I've discovered this great resource where you can see fifty-five of them: https://www.jesusfilm.org/blog-and-stories/old-testament-prophecies.html.

Chapter 8
The Encounters

As I have pressed into things "Jewish," I have met many other Jewish friends who have embraced Yeshua as their Messiah. Some encounters are more profound and supernatural than others, like Jonathan Degrenier's story.

Jonathan was a sixteen-year-old drug dealer, trying to make quick money so he didn't have to work a nine-to-five job. One night his supplier asked to meet, which was odd, because Jonathan usually conducted his exchanges with this man during daylight hours. When Jonathan entered the meeting place, a PT Cruiser, he saw the supplier on the right, and *his* boss on the left, in the driver's seat. "I could feel the air shift in the car as I took a seat in the back and knew I wasn't coming out alive. I began to pray silently. *G-d, please protect my family and tell my brothers that I love them.*

Jonathan's parents were divorced—his father, a strong Catholic and his mother a devout Jew. So, religiously, it was a divided household even before the two parents parted ways. Because he lived with his mother, Jonathan was brought up in the synagogue. "We would be there Sunday, Wednesday, and Friday. I remember going straight from school to religious school or Jewish studies, where we'd learn Hebrew, History, and Holidays of our people. Looking back, I think our home was comparable to most Jewish children's upbringing. We never missed a Sabbath for lighting the candles or gathering around for Chanukah, spinning dreidels or making Tzedakah boxes. One of my favorite memories growing up was my mother singing Hashkiveinu and the Shema to us right before going to bed."

Meanwhile, Jonathan's dad had married a very devout Christian named Jodi, who was in love with G-d and Yeshua. On the weekends, he'd often stay with his dad and Jodi. It was during those stretches at his dad's home that Jodi began to open Jonathan's mind to the supernatural aspect of G-d and the possibility that Yeshua was indeed the Son of G-d.

One day Jodi and Jonathan were walking down a path in a trailer park when Jodi asked Jonathan to do something bizarre. "She told me to dig in a pile of leaves on the path, because there would be money for food at the bottom of the pile, and assured me that is what G-d told her to instruct me to do." Jonathan's family did not have any food and needed the cash, so he was willing to try anything. "Sure enough, I ravaged through the leaves, and G-d provided more than what we could have asked for."

That was the first of three miracles Jonathan experienced in his youth, two of which involved Jodi. Another time, as a twelve-year-old boy, he had an infection in his foot. The infection changed the pigmentation as it spread up to his ankle. It was bad enough that it was probably going to require a hospital visit. "I was scared, but not Jodi. She laid her hands on the open cut and said, 'In Jesus's name, be whole,' and just like that I watched my pigmentation return to normal color and the infection slowly recede until my skin was normal again. The cut completely disappeared."

So as Jonathan sat in the back of the putrid colored vehicle, facing certain death, he prayed for a miracle, "G-d of my fathers, I know you're real; but Jesus if you're real, make yourself known now and get me out of this situation and I'll serve you forever." Less than thirty seconds after Jonathan said that in his heart, there was a breakthrough. The boss on the driver's side released a heavy breath of air. A sigh followed, and he said, "I don't know what's coming over me but I'm going to let you go. I'm leaving the country, and if the feds ever find me, I will know it was one of you who snitched. You've made me some good money, and now I'm letting you go." Then it was Jonathan who breathed a sigh of relief. He never looked back and never sold drugs again. "I committed myself to Yeshua and I'm always grateful to Him for intervening in that moment."

Jonathan has seen miraculous changes in his life since that defining rescue. "I'm more tender and able to show grace. I've learned how to love and how to forgive—to love unconditionally. I had to forgive my older brother for some inappropriate things he did with my little brother. When he asked for my forgiveness. I chose love. I chose Christ."

Today, Jonathan serves by assisting churches with tech help. He moves from church-to-church until they have established tech teams to help the pastors in ministry. He also runs a ministry that provides single mothers throughout the Dallas-Ft. Worth area with food and clothing. "I just give and serve wherever the L-RD needs me."

Carolyn Margolin Hyde also had a supernatural encounter with Yeshua. She grew up in a traditional Orthodox Jewish synagogue near Chicago. Her father owned a shmata (clothing) business where she helped out; and her dad was the president of the synagogue, so she and her family were at every Shabbat and observed all of the Feasts of the L-RD found in Leviticus 23. "I loved growing up Jewish—it was very family oriented," said Carolyn. "I remember at Pesach we'd gather with the family and closest friends for a Seder. My mom had a gift of hospitality and cared about the widows and the singles in our community; so every Erev Shabbat our home was filled with widows and elderly people sitting around the table. I loved it, but I think my dad preferred to not always have so much company!"

But Carolyn's memories of Gentiles were not so pleasant. "We never hosted Gentiles in our home. We had a cleaning lady who was Gentile, and sometimes we'd call on a plumber or a home repair service, but we never ate together. I also remember during the Easter season, kids at school would throw rocks at my brothers and me, calling us 'Christ-killers.' When we asked our parents about this, they said that Christians hate Jews so we should just stay away from them. So I did."

But for a while Carolyn lost her way. In high school she became rebellious, and in her searching she looked into the New Age Movement. She tried everything possible, but nothing satisfied and nothing seemed to matter. "Depression set in while I was in university; and after I graduated, I went to Mexico and Central America to sing the blues in bars."

It was while Carolyn was south of the border that she had two unexplainable experiences that changed her life forever. The first was in Guatemala. "I was traveling with a group of ten other hippies, singing in clubs and just hanging out a lot. One day I wandered off from the youth hostel and walked about two hours north. While [I was] in a restaurant, a man approached me and asked, 'Do you really know who you are?' That scared me so much that I took off running, and within one minute, I was in front of my youth hostel and I had no idea how that happened! But later after coming to faith, when I read 1 Kings 18:46, that says, 'The power of the L-RD came on Elijah and, tucking his cloak into his belt, he ran ahead of Ahab all the way to Jezreel,' it became my favorite Scripture."

After more experiences in Guatemala, including a scary encounter with a corrupt policeman, Carolyn made her way to Cancun. She did not stay at a fancy hotel resort but lived in town, in a hut with local natives. Perhaps the elimination of distractions and embracing a simpler way of life created the atmosphere for what would happen next. It was in Cancun where Carolyn had a divine visitation, not unlike the one patriarchs Abraham or Moses had when they came face-to-face with the Angel of the L-RD.

"I had a vision; angels were singing with me while I played the piano. I remember looking up and seeing Yeshua—Jesus. Something that was stuck on my eyes fell off and I remember that Yeshua was dressed in shining white clothes with a golden sash. His eyes saw right through me, eyes full of such compassion as I'd never seen before and instantly I declared, 'It's Jesus and He is the L-RD!' And then I realized that this was dangerous to say, so I became a secret believer."

After returning to America, Carolyn began work as a nurse. "During my four years alone, the thought never even occurred to me to attend a church because I figured Jews don't go to church." But she did grow spiritually during that time, because as a home health nurse, she had seven African-American patients who were pastors or elders in their churches, and they all discipled her.

Eventually, Carolyn became more vocal about her faith; and after marrying, she made a long-distance move to Israel, where she serves in full-time ministry in Haifa with her sons, Ariel and Avi. Through Heartofg-d Ministries (heartofg-d.org), Carolyn and her family share Messiah on the streets and make outreach videos and music videos to post on social media sites. "Yeshua completely changed my life from one of doubt and fear to one of confidence in Messiah," said Carolyn. "I now have joy in His presence."

Kim Kingsriter has a story similar to mine, as she was brought back to her Jewish roots as an adult. Kim's paternal grandmother was half-Jewish but no one knew this until after she had died.

In the meantime, Kim was brought up in an affluent, yet dysfunctional home. On the outside, it looked like a typical American family. On the inside, not so much. Kim said, "There was alcoholism, yelling, cussing, abuse, and a divorce by the time I was ten. We would go to church on Christmas, Easter, and a few times in between to try to look like a wholesome family, but none of us had a personal relationship with Yeshua. It was just a religious act."

Kim ended up in a similar environment in her marriage; but by that time she had a one-year-old daughter, a fourteen-year-old stepson, and an eighty-seven year old grandmother living with them in their large, comfortable home. "I was so miserable that I started going by myself to a marriage counselor and made a decision to give it all up, get a divorce, and move back to Dallas. My older sister, Deb, was born again about ten years before I was. She would tell me that G-d was good and that He loved me."

The very morning that Kim made the final counseling appointment in Nashville to end her marriage, she made a lunch date with her new neighbor. "She surprised me when she asked if I minded skipping lunch and just talking instead. She said she was fasting and praying for one of our neighbors who was dying of cancer. To my surprise, the first question out of my mouth was 'How did you get so religious?' I thought it was a club she had joined—I was clueless."

Kim's neighbor then began to share her story, and told Kim she could be "born again" too. "She told me I didn't have to clean myself up to come to Jesus, but when I come to Jesus, He cleans me up. I said I thought that might work then." Kim prayed a prayer to receive Yeshua right there on her couch and was radically transformed that day. She began learning about G-d and Yeshua by attending Bible studies. Then, after a move to Denver, she enrolled at Marilyn Hickey's Bible College. One of the classes she took was "Old Testament Feasts and Tabernacle."

"As I am sitting in class this one particular day an intense heat came over my chest area. I was too young for hot flashes so I knew it wasn't that. I asked the Holy Spirit under my breath what it was. He said it was passion. I said, 'passion for what?' He said, 'This! Passion for Israel and the Jewish roots of your faith. Passion to teach what you are learning here.'"

Three years after moving to Denver, Kim and her family relocated to Orlando, where she attended a conference called "Israel Encounter." "I am sitting at a banquet table with Jews and Christians—I couldn't be more confused. I thought, *We don't like each other*. However, when the Messianic worship started, my natural Jewish DNA came alive with my spiritual DNA and that is where I fell in love with Israel and the Jewish people. I had a revelation of G-d's love for His people." Soon after this happened, Kim began teaching the Jewish roots of the Christian faith and has been teaching this for the past twenty five years.

Greg Rosenberg is also grateful for G-d's divine intervention in his life. "I did a lot of things I'm not proud of today, and no doubt I should not be alive today."

Greg grew up in a conservative Jewish home in St. Louis, Missouri, the son of Ashkenazic Jews. His mother kept a kosher home (no pork or shellfish, two sets of dishes, two different ovens). "We celebrated most Jewish holidays, went to synagogue many Sabbaths and for all the high holidays, always had a Passover Seder. We also celebrated Shabbat every Friday evening with lighting the candles, saying bruchas, and eating a Shabbat meal, which included Shabbat Dunkin' Donuts. Every Passover, my family came together for a Seder at our house."

However, just before Greg's Bar Mitzvah, his parents divorced and he went to live with his friends. It was then that his destructive lifestyle began. "During this time in my life, I prayed to G-d mostly when I needed something or when I promised to stop doing stupid things."

After seeking some structure through a stint in the Air Force, Greg fulfilled his Air Force commitment and returned to St. Louis, where he began working at McDonnell Douglas, building F-15's. Meanwhile, his faith was like a grounded plane. As an adult, Greg still believed in G-d, but the idea of having a personal relationship with Him seemed like an impossibility. "I figured G-d was too busy running the universe to care about me personally," said Greg.

One day an inspector at McDonnell Douglas named Walter Joyce approached Greg and asked what he thought about Isaiah 53. Greg replied, "'I don't recall what it says' (as if I once did). Walter then invited me to read Isaiah 53 in his Bible at break time, but I declined the offer. I told Walter, 'When I get home, I'll take a look at my Tanak and read it and get back to you.' I wasn't serious, but it seemed like a good way to end the conversation."

Greg was eventually laid off from McDonnell Douglas but applied for a program going on in Saudi Arabia to upgrade F-15's. "No Jews were allowed in Saudi Arabia, and I was told that none of my documentation could hint I was Jewish, so I had to get state-certified documents. My family was not excited I was going to Saudi Arabia, but I felt the money was too good to pass up and I was responsible for supporting my family."

Once Greg and his family arrived in Saudi Arabia, he surveyed the social environment and discovered two types of American groups working on the F-15 program: the party people and the Christians. "I understood the party people, but by now I had a young daughter and I didn't want my kids hanging around with parents who cursed a lot and whose morals went against the changes I was making in my own life."

Greg found the Christians to be very different. They seemed happier, like they knew something he didn't. They were mannered differently. "They had this community thing going on, they worked hard and didn't seem to gossip like the other group. Their children were well-behaved, and so I wanted my daughter to play with their daughters. I didn't mind hanging out with them; I just didn't want their Jesus."

Eventually, Greg's new group invited him to a Bible study where they were studying Leviticus, part of the Torah. He was curious enough to attend and found out they knew more about Leviticus than most Jewish people he knew. Greg began asking a lot of questions. "They went to the verses that addressed my questions and they also told me what they thought; but then they said, 'You have to read and make up your own mind.'"

For the first time in Greg's life, he became interested in studying the Bible for himself. He read the Tanak cover to cover in a few months. "I discovered a lot of things I thought, and was told, were either different than what the Bible says, or not supported by the Tanak. Realizing this, I then put the Bible on trial because I needed to be sure I could rely on what it said was true." He said, "I examined many evidences for the authenticity of the Bible (historical, scientific, prophetic, archeological) and was overwhelmed at all there was. I wondered why we had never discussed these things. I was also amazed at all the prophecies that spoke about the Messiah.

Why didn't any of my Rabbis even talk about Messiah—really talk about Him?"

After reading the Tanak, Greg decided to read one book from the New Testament, the gospel of John, and was surprised to find out it had been written by a Jewish person and was very "Jewish." "I wasn't sure Jesus was the Messiah, but I had no problem with the things He said and things He did. So I decided to read the whole New Testament. I felt like the New Testament explained things the Old did not. I learned 'Old' does not mean done away with, but is referring to two different covenants made with the Jewish people. Gentiles were clearly included in the New Covenant, which made sense to me, because G-d loves all people."

After eight months of Bible study, questions, evidences, and prayer asking the L-RD to show him the truth, Greg ran out of excuses to *not* believe Yeshua is the Jewish Messiah. One day an evangelist came to their compound in Saudi Arabia, and Greg went to hear him speak. He preached on Jonah and highlighted sin and repentance. By this time, Greg realized if he died, he wasn't going to make it to heaven due to his sins and the lack of a blood sacrifice, according to the Torah, so he knew he had to make a decision.

"So I stood up during the meeting and said 'I need to be baptized.' The words just seemed to come out of my mouth without any hesitation. Others stood up too. I got in the water and people were crying. (I actually thought they were going to drown me.) A friend welcomed me into G-d's family and I got choked up. I later officially asked Jesus to be my L-RD and Messiah and never felt more Jewish in my whole life. I knew I was following the Jewish scriptures and found that G-d wanted a personal relationship."

Greg now serves G-d as a Jewish pastor at Gateway Church in Southlake, Texas. He concludes, "There are some who say I am no longer Jewish because I believe in Jesus. I'm very content to let G-d define my Jewishness. For me, the main issue is not whether or not I am Jewish. The more important question is, 'Who is Jesus?'"

I'll end this chapter with a "high profile" Jewish testimony that I heard two years ago. In 2018, I attended the National Religious Broadcasters Convention in Nashville, Tennessee; and while there as "working media," I had the privilege of interviewing Rabbi Jonathan Cahn, best-selling author of *The Harbinger, The Mystery of the Shemitah, The Paradigm,* and *The Oracle,* to name a few. Cahn was raised in a Reformed Jewish home. As a young boy, his father escaped Hitler. He was sent out on a train, ultimately arriving in America. His mother's family escaped the Czar in Russia. Rabbi Cahn has deep Jewish roots; and in my radio interview, conducted with co-host, Donna Skell, we asked Cahn to share his story of how he came to a belief in Yeshua as the Messiah. The following is the transcript from that portion of the interview.

> I was raised going to synagogue, and both my parents were scientists, so it wasn't a very religious home. But when I was eight years old, I questioned it all and I

125

said, "How do we know there is a G-d?" and I
became an atheist in the synagogue. When I was
twelve or thirteen, I started thinking there has to be
something—we can't be here for no reason—so I
started seeking every form of truth I could imagine,
getting books in science, religion, the occult, UFO's,
everything. One day I picked up a book. I thought it
was a UFO book, but it was *The Late Great Planet
Earth* by Hal Lyndsey, all about biblical prophecy
coming true. I had no idea, so I'm telling my friends
about it. Now I wasn't a believer and I'm telling my
friends and I'm winning them to the L-RD. And so
finally I knew I had to give my life to the L-RD; but I
didn't want to give my life to the L-RD, because I
thought if I give my life to the L-RD, you give up
everything that's good—*and you know I had a rock band.*
I had all these things as a teenager and I didn't want
to give anything up. So I made a deal with G-d. "If
you give me a long life, I'll accept you when I'm on
my death bed."

So right after that, I almost got killed twice. The
first time was a car accident. The second time I'm in a
Ford Pinto heading to a train track at night and
there's a light. People have been crossing the track
but the light was going on, so I thought *Maybe it's
broken.* So I'm going up—and it's a dangerous thing—
there was no protection. You couldn't even tell where
you were because it was on an angle. I look and I see
a light to my left. It was a train and it didn't look like
it was moving because I was right on the track and it
was coming at me. So I said to be safe let me back up
a little bit. I look and there are headlights in back of
me. The train's coming I have somebody in back of
me so I backed up about a foot. I thought I was just

being extra safe. I was still in the path of the train. The train came, smashed into the Ford Pinto; it went up like aluminum foil and the only thing I could do was call out to G-d. The car was destroyed. I didn't get a scratch. I said, "L-RD, can we renegotiate. New deal. I'll accept you when I turn twenty. Just don't kill me until then."

So on my twentieth birthday, like a man whose contract had run out, I didn't know how to get saved. I was reading the Bible. I was listening to Christian radio, but I didn't know how to get saved. I remember in Hebrew school, G-d met Moses on a mountain, Elijah on a mountain; so let me find a mountain. I found a mountain. I went up to the top of the mountain that night, kneeled down on a rock and gave my life to the L-RD. It's said that Jews demand signs. I needed a train."

Chapter 9
The Grafting

One of the most interesting aspects of the Messianic movement is that it's not just Jews or individuals with Jewish roots who attend a Messianic congregation. It's my experience that a great majority are non-Jews who have a heart for Israel and believe, because of the chosen ones and the message G-d delivered through them, they are "grafted in" to this special relationship that G-d has with Israel.

This idea of Gentiles being grafted into the family of G-d was first discussed by the apostle Paul in Romans 11:11–24. Since many Jewish people did not accept Yeshua as the Messiah during His three-year ministry, that created an opening for Gentiles to enter this union with G-d through faith in Yeshua, resulting in eternal salvation. Paul inferred this should not lead to any arrogance among Gentiles, but rather, a humble acceptance of this gift. Paul said in verses 17-18, "But if some of the branches were broken off and you—being a wild olive—were grafted in among them and became a partaker of the root of the olive tree with its richness, do not boast against the branches. But if you do boast, it is not you who support the root but the root supports you." Paul goes on to say in Romans 11:25-26, that Israel has experienced a hardening in part until the full number of Gentiles has come in, and "in this way all Israel will be saved."

Pastor and author Jack Wellman gives an explanation of this passage: "The branches that were broken off are clearly those Jews who have rejected Christ, but this broken branch allows the *'wild olive shoot'* to be grafted into the natural olive tree, or the nation of Israel; therefore we should not be *'arrogant towards the branches'* of the natural olive tree (Israel) but thankful that we who were outside of the family of G-d can now become part of that tree." He goes on to say, "Don't despise the Jews because they were the root that supports us by their holding onto the Holy Scriptures."[xxxix]

I believe the time of the Gentiles is nearing the end, as we are seeing more sons and daughters of Abraham recognizing Yeshua as Messiah than ever before. In 1999, there were about 5,000 Messianic Jews living in Israel, and now there are estimated 15,000 Jewish believers there, a 200 percent increase in twenty years.[xl]

Ingrid Anderson, director of Jewish Studies at Boston University, has done some research about the number of Jewish believers in the US. She says there are approximately 175,000 to 250,000 Messianic Jews living in the United States, and 350,000 worldwide. There are currently about 300 Messianic congregations in the US; however, about half of the attendants are Gentiles, with no Jewish heritage whatsoever.[xli]

So what draws the non-Jew to things Jewish? Why do people gravitate toward Jewish customs and observances and have a love for Israel? In this chapter, we'll share a number of accounts from Gentile believers who have embraced the Jewish people and G-d's plan for Israel.

Sue is one of those Gentiles who now serves in Jewish ministries at her church. She grew up in New York, and many orthodox Jews lived in her area. She would ask, "Why are they dressed so differently?" Sue's father worked for a Jewish man at an insurance company. "When my father was stressed about something at work, I would often hear him talking with my mother, using disrespectful remarks about Jews and how they were so tight with money! This confused me, because his boss was a kind man. Often, on Saturdays, he would stop by with papers for my dad to sign and he would smoke a cherry-flavored cigar. From my room I would smell it and race downstairs to be greeted with his Donald Duck impersonation. He was the best!"

Right before Sue gave her heart to Yeshua in the early 80s, she attended a Bible study where the leader had a heart for the Jewish people. "As I would listen to her teaching, I'd watch tears stream down her face as she prayed for Jewish people and for Israel. I was so confused. My father's words came flooding back to my memory. I look back at that time and feel like the L-RD was positioning my past and my future to collide."

A short time later, Sue became a Christian believer and started attending a church in Nashville, Tennessee, where Don Finto was the pastor. Sue's father had recently died, and Don became a spiritual father to Sue and her husband, who had lost his father as well. "Don had a big heart and became involved with the newly developing Messianic movement in the late eighties. I watched Don become an activist for reconciliation between the Jews and Gentiles, in a time when they were very separate."

Finto has since written several books, including *Your People Shall Be My People* and *God's Promise and the Future of Israel.* Finto's love of Israel and the Jewish people rubbed off on Sue and her husband Pete. After moving to Texas in 2006, they began attending Messianic services at Gateway Church in Southlake, Texas, and now oversee the prayer team for Jewish Ministries. Their love for the Jewish people and Israel continue to grow.

Nestor Lima also has a heart for the Jewish people, but not before walking a very dark road as a teenager. He was involved in gangs, sold drugs, and participated in all of the shady things that coincide with that type of lifestyle. This journey into dangerous territory occurred even though Nestor's parents raised him in the church, first as a Catholic, then as an evangelical. At age 19, Nestor had a radical encounter with Jesus, which transformed his life in many different ways. According to Nestor, "It led me

132

in a path of love for G-d and people. Less than a year later, I began preaching and teaching the Word of G-d. It has been an incredible experience since then."

Growing up, Nestor doesn't remember having anything to do with Jewish people; but he does recall the stereotypes and prejudices against them, which he says is still common in the Hispanic culture. "My mother, however, always instilled respect toward the Jews," said Nestor, "'because they are the chosen people of G-d,' she would say. She encouraged my siblings and me to bless Israel and the Jewish people."

After preaching for over twenty years, Nestor's eyes were opened when he ministered at a Messianic congregation in Buenos Aires and had what he calls an "encounter with Yeshua." "Though it was my first 'Jewish' experience, I felt like I was home. Everyone was praising, dancing, and loving on Yeshua. The presence and love of G-d filled the environment. After I preached that night and the service was concluded, some people gathered to greet me and asked for prayer. G-d touched each person in a special way. One after another they came. When all was done at about 4:00 a.m., I left the building to catch a flight back to the States, just three hours later. I felt my soul had bonded with my Messianic brothers and sisters. This experience launched me on a path to learn more about my faith from a Jewish perspective. It was after this event that I came to the understanding of being "grafted" into the olive tree.

After his encounter in Buenos Aires, Nestor says the Holy Spirit convicted him of anti-Semitism. Since then his love for the Jews and Israel has been kindled and his overall understanding of the Jewish roots of his faith has increased. As a result, Nestor and his oldest daughter traveled to Israel in 2014. To understand the Jewish people better, he and his daughter took a two-week cultural immersion trip where they lived among the people, rented cars and apartments, and used public transportation.

Nestor did not stop there. To be better equipped to serve, he enrolled at the School of Messianic Theology, affiliated with the Messianic Jewish Bible Institute (MJB), and graduated in May 2020. He and his wife Dina lead Havdalah classes at Gateway Church's North Richland Hills Campus, and they've overseen a Shabbat group together for the last three years.

After another journey to the Holy Land, Nestor came up with an additional outreach. "During our family trip to Israel in 2018, the L-RD gave me an idea to combat anti-Semitism within the Hispanic Christian culture. Hence, "IsraelAhora.com" was born to reach Spanish speaking congregations with a healthy Biblical view about Israel and the Jewish people. A special element of Israel Ahora includes Messianic trips to Israel that culminate with a "Reconnected Event" held in Jerusalem, which consists of worshiping with local Messianic Jews and encouraging reconciliation between Jewish believers and Gentile Christians. The overall purpose of Israel Ahora is to:

- **Reconnect** Gentile believers to the Jewish roots of their Christian faith
- **Reconcile** the Church and Messianic Jews
- **Rediscover** the blessings of our spiritual heritage
- **Renew** a tangible love and support for Israel and the Jewish people

Nestor's mother, who encouraged him to bless the Jewish people so many years ago, would be proud.

It wasn't until Nestor's wife Dina was in her forties that she came to an understanding about being grafted into the commonwealth of Israel. Dina was brought up in a Christian home in the small town of Santa Rosa de Lima in El Salvador, Central America, the daughter of a preaching evangelist. Her mother taught her to have a love for G-d's Word and encouraged her to memorize verses and Psalms that she still remembers to this day. "Jesus said the truth sets us free. Understanding the Jewishness of Jesus and the Bible has enriched my personal walk with G-d," said Dina. "I have greater appreciation for the Jewish people and all they have suffered as a ransom nation for the entire world, a beacon to all peoples, pointing them to the One True G-d." One of the ways Dina shows her love for Israel is by increasing her knowledge of their history through the Bible and other books. "In addition, I stand up for Israel in conversations with others," Dina said. "It's a way to deflect anti-Semitic comments that even believers unknowingly make."

Susan is another who came to an understanding of the important role the Jewish people play in the history of Christianity. She lived all over the world as a child—including Saigon, Vietnam and Yalova, Turkey. She also spent an extended time in Ras Tanura, Saudi Arabia, where her engineer father moved the family for two years. Her family attended church occasionally and was not particularly religious.

Susan had her first encounter with Jewish people when she was a teenager. A Jewish doctor and his family were hosting a Fourth of July party for a large group of friends. They needed help with set-up, serving guests, and clean-up. According to Susan, "Two things that impressed me were that they seemed to possess a strong, cohesive sense of family and community, and most seemed to be very successful."

But Susan experienced two life-changing events where she came to an understanding of being "grafted in" to the Christian faith because of G-d's revelation to the Jews. She came to faith in the L-RD Jesus Christ; and at nineteen, she participated in a missions-sponsored experience to serve Jewish people on two kibbutzim (collectively owned and run communities) in Israel for two years. From the experiences of meeting Jewish people, serving in Israel, Bible study, and strong Scriptural teaching, Susan grew in her understanding of G-d's love for, favor of, and future plan for Israel and the Jewish people. "I can only describe it as a G-d-given love," said Susan. "I have a strong passion for Israel and the Jewish people. Rarely a day passes, when hearing of

136

issues affecting Israel or the Jews that my heart isn't moved. Issues may involve politics, the BDS movement (a Palestinian-led campaign for boycotting Israel), the rise in global anti-Semitism, Jews making Aliyah (immigration) to Israel, prophetic-related news about the coming third Temple in Jerusalem——[they all] stir me."

Susan is studying Hebrew, learning about the Levitical feasts of the L-RD, and defending the place and priority of the Jews. She believes G-d meant it when He said in Genesis 12:2, "I will bless those who bless you and curse those who treat you with contempt. All the families on earth will be blessed through you." She demonstrates this by supporting projects that benefit local Jewish ministries and by participating in mission trips to Israel to help Holocaust survivors. She is also countering the philosophy of "replacement theology" among Christians. Replacement theology, Susan says, "is 'the belief that the whole or part of the Abrahamic Covenant has been abolished.' It is this covenant that promises to Israel eternal ownership of the land of Canaan (Genesis 17:7–8). Once this 'promise' has been removed, the present-day restoration of Israel means nothing, and her only hope is in the Church."xlii

This covenant between G-d and His chosen ones was first established in Genesis 15. In verse 9, *ADONAI* asks the patriarch Abram to bring him a three-year-old young cow, a three-year-old she-goat, a three-year-old ram, a turtle-dove, and a young bird. Abram located them, then cut them in half and put each piece opposite the other; but he did not cut the birds. When Abram fell into a deep sleep, *ADONAI* said this to him: "Know for certain that your seed will be strangers in a land that is not theirs, and they will be enslaved and oppressed 400 years. But I am going to judge the nation that they will serve. Afterward they will go out with many possessions. But you, you will come to your fathers in peace. You will be buried at a good old age. Then in the fourth generation they will return here—for the iniquity of the Amorites is not yet complete" (Genesis 15:13–16). When the sun set and it became dark, a smoking oven and a fiery torch passed between the pieces, and that is when *ADONAI* cut the covenant with Abram, saying, "I give this land to your seed, from the river of Egypt to the great river, the Euphrates River: the Kenite, the Kenizzites, the Kadmonites, the Hittites, the Perizzites, the Raphaites, the Amorites, the Canaanites, the Girgashites, and the Jebusites" (Genesis 15:18–21).

In Genesis 17, *ADONAI* made a return visit to Abram, now 99 years old. He renamed Abram "Abraham," which means "father of many" and added to the covenant already established. He told Abraham he would be the father of many nations and said, "I will establish My covenant between Me and you and your seed after you throughout their generations for an everlasting covenant, in order to be your God and your seed's God after you." At that point, Abraham and his wife Sarai, renamed Sarah, had no children to carry on into the generations, but *ADONAI* promised him and his wife a son in their old age. That son would be named Isaac. The sign of this covenant was circumcision of the flesh of the foreskin, a constant reminder of the everlasting agreement with *ADONAI*.

This all happened before *ADONAI* gave the law to Moses; after receipt of the law, circumcision became a heart issue as well as a physical act of obedience. Deuteronomy 30:6 says, "Also *ADONAI* will circumcise your heart and the heart of your descendants—to love *ADONAI* your God with all your heart and with all your soul, in order that you may live." The apostle Paul echoes this in Romans 2:

> Circumcision is indeed worthwhile if you keep the *Torah*; but if you break the *Torah*, your circumcision has become uncircumcision. Therefore, if the uncircumcised keeps the righteous decrees of the *Torah*, will not his uncircumcision be counted as circumcision? Indeed, the one not circumcised physically who fulfills the *Torah* will judge you who— even with the written code and circumcision—break the *Torah*. For one is not a Jew who is one outwardly, nor is circumcision something visible in the flesh. Rather, the Jew is one inwardly, and circumcision is of the heart—in Spirit not in letter. His praise is not from men, but from God (Romans 2: 25–29).

And that is where the "New Covenant" comes in, prophesied in the book of Jeremiah.

"Behold, days are coming"—it is a declaration of *ADONAI*—"when I will make a new covenant with the house of Israel and with the house of Judah—not like the covenant I made with their fathers in the day I took them by the hand to bring them out of the land of Egypt. For they broke My covenant, though I was a husband to them." It is a declaration of *ADONAI*. "But this is the covenant I will make with the house of Israel after those days" —it is a declaration of *ADONAI*—"I will put My Torah within them. Yes, I will write it on their heart" (Jeremiah 31:30–32).

In Romans 2:15–16, the apostle Paul confirms that the law is now written on our hearts when we accept Yeshua as part of this "New Covenant." "They show that the work of the *Torah* is written in their hearts, their conscience bearing witness and their thoughts switching between accusing or defending them on the day when God judges the secrets of men according to my Good News through Messiah *Yeshua*."

So if *ADONAI* does the heart work through Yeshua, then what is our part? According to Robert Friedman in his article, "Circumcision of the Heart," it's repentance. He says we find the answer in Leviticus 26::

But if they confess their iniquity and that of their fathers, in the treachery they committed against Me, and how they walked contrary to Me —in return I walked contrary to them and brought them into the land of their enemies—and if at that time their uncircumcised heart becomes humbled, so that they accept the punishment for their iniquity, then I will remember My covenant with Jacob and also My covenant with Isaac and My covenant with Abraham, and I will remember the land (Leviticus 26:40–42).

Friedman goes on to explain that once we confess our sins, then G-d does the rest. "This appears to be a spiritual operation, but we sense within ourselves that we lack the divine power necessary to perform this—to change our own heart. Then we remember this is an operation G-d said He would perform."[xliii]

I often pray Psalm 51:10 over myself in the morning, "Create in me a pure heart, O God and renew a steadfast spirit within me." Philippians 4:13 promises, "I can do all things through Messiah who strengthens me." I know I need help for my circumcised heart to be pleasing to *ADONAI*. This assurance comes courtesy of the New Covenant that Yeshua ushered in.

My dear prayer partner and gifted artist Debbie Jackson, who provided the cover art for this book, has recently created a series of paintings based on G-d's covenant with His people. Debbie, a Gentile, has always had a deep love for anyone who told her they were Jewish. She's felt that way her entire life. "When my grandparents were celebrating their fiftieth wedding anniversary in 1977, my dad and his siblings gifted them with tickets to visit and experience the Holy Land. It was a lifelong dream of theirs, and it became a lifelong desire of my heart." However, Debbie did not receive her invitation to Israel until the fall of 2016. She and her husband David walked through the historical places documented in the Bible, where Yeshua performed many miracles in the Creator's land. "After our trip to Israel, I prayed and asked the L-RD about what

He wanted me to do with the photo images that we took while on the trip. A prophecy spoken over me two days after we returned was that the L-RD would reveal His covenant to me."

Debbie then studied the word "covenant," and the story came into focus about how she could share her journey with others. She saw that G-d promised that all of the nations of the world would be blessed through the seed and lineage of Abraham, Isaac, and Jacob, who was renamed "Israel" by the Creator.

So from the end of 2016 through 2017, Debbie began to artistically portray the covenant G-d made with His people. "My time was invested in painting the twenty-nine original oil paintings to walk a person through several scenes in Israel, along with providing scriptures written in 'soundbites' or paraphrased from the King James Version of the Bible." She documented it all in a book titled, *Eternal Perspective: Connecting the Crimson Dots of His Covenant.* Debbie's book and accompanying painting exhibit were designed to travel and share the good news of Yeshua through words and visual images. The first museum exhibit was launched at the Museum of Biblical Art in Dallas, Texas.

Debbie was able to return to Israel in the spring of 2019 and hopes to make many more visits. "Our hearts are to bless the people of Israel, however the L-RD puts it on our hearts to do so. We love our Jewish friends and neighbors very much, and look forward to returning to Israel as many times as the L-RD grants us to go before our time on this earth expires or He returns—whatever comes first."

142

Chapter 10
The Tribe

There is an unmistakable connection between believers in Yeshua. It's provided by the Holy Spirit within us, but I also believe there is an inexplicable bond between those who have Jewish blood running through their veins. I believe it's a tribal connection, but for many years I did not know which tribe the "Adler" family emerged from.

The subject of "tribes" came up one mild, sunny day in San Antonio, Texas. I was sitting outside on a restaurant patio, enjoying lunch with my Jewish friend Amy, and I asked her, "Do you know what tribe you are from?" She said, "I don't know, but I bet my dad does." So Amy, perhaps curious herself, called her father and asked him the question. In a split second, he replied, "Benjamin. Who wants to know?" She explained that I was curious, and he then said, "Tell Lisa that knowing her tribe is not as important as what she is doing now with her Jewish faith." Some wise words from Mr. Weinstein.

However, I had a "need to know" and still desired to discover my tribe. For years, I thought my Jewish roots went back to the half-tribe of "Manasseh" because of my great uncle, Manasseh. Manasseh, as told in the book of Genesis, was Joseph's older son, who was known for receiving less of a blessing than his younger brother Ephraim. When it came time for their grandfather and patriarch Jacob to issue the blessing, Joseph took his sons to see him. Jacob first adopted the boys as his own, then crossed his arms and put his right hand on Ephraim and his left on the older Manasseh. Joseph was disturbed by this and said, "'Not like that, my father, because this one's the firstborn. Put your right hand upon his head.' But his father refused and said, 'I know, my son, I know. He also will become a people, and he also will become great. But his younger brother will become greater than he and his seed will be the fullness of the nations'" (Genesis 48:18-19).

Maybe Jacob didn't like Manasseh's name. Ephraim's name means "fruitful" in Hebrew and Manasseh's "one that makes to forget." Joseph said he gave him that name because "God has caused me to forget all my trouble and all my father's house" (Genesis 41:51).

So what did Joseph want to forget? This son of Jacob, as you probably know from your early Torah teaching, was sold into slavery by his jealous brothers. After they betrayed him, they dipped Joseph's tunic in goat's blood, then showed the tunic to their father Jacob, asking if he recognized it. Of

144

course, he recognized it. Jacob immediately knew whose tunic it was, and thought a wild animal had torn Joseph apart, so he began to mourn the loss of his child. Years later, Joseph, his brothers, and his dad were reunited, but not until after Joseph endured slavery and a prison sentence based on false charges. It was Joseph's spot-on dream interpretation that gave him a "get-out-of-jail-free" card; after interpreting Pharaoh's dreams, Joseph was elevated to second-in-command in Egypt. During a time of famine in Israel, the scheming brothers came to Egypt looking for food, and it was Joseph who was able to help them. Through this scenario, the family was eventually reunited and Joseph forgave his brothers. He realized why the hard times had to happen, to save his people—your people and my people. (How was that for a synopsis?)

Let's turn the corner back to Manasseh; there seemed to be some correlation between Manasseh's name and what I myself had gone through in life—my own rejection by family members—so being from the tribe of Manasseh made sense to me.

I also thought, because of my heart for ministry, that it wouldn't be a far stretch to say my tribe could be Levi. After all, they were the tribe of priests, and for many years they served at the tabernacle or the Temple. However, once I found out there were ten *lost* tribes—those tribes from the Northern Kingdom of Israel who were exiled to Mesopotamia and the Medes (modern Syria and Iraq today) and never seen again—my search narrowed down to Benjamin or Judah.

I got tired of trying to guess and finally consulted my Jewish cousin Frank (pseudo name), who has compiled the genealogy for the Adler family. He didn't know our tribal roots, but he said he would ask his son, "who knows all things Jewish." He got back to me and said, "To the best of my son's knowledge, the Adler family is from the tribe of Judah." Now that was a curve ball. Judah? Well, that's Yeshua's tribe. It's also King David's tribe. Now I can say I descended from royalty!

I had met Frank via email years before I asked this question. He and his family had relocated from California to a Florida resort area, near Miami, and I said, "If I ever make it to Miami, I will come meet you in person." One day my husband said he had to go to Miami for a client meeting and asked, "Do you want to go?" I thought, *It's my chance to meet Frank!* So we made a family vacation out of it. My husband and youngest son went fishing, and my oldest son and I went up to Frank's gated neighborhood to meet him and his family. It happened to be Passover weekend. We had a beautiful lunch together. Frank's son and his girlfriend were in town to conduct the Seder at their neighborhood country club. I did not hide the fact that I was a believer in Yeshua, and I left behind some of the Christian books I had written. In retrospect, that was probably a no-no.

After I returned home, I noticed my name had disappeared from the genealogy website and was listed as "private." Communication with Frank basically stopped, and I came to the conclusion that I had been rejected by Jewish family members again.

146

While it stung, G-d still would not let me walk away from this heritage.

What I've grown to realize is that while family members may shun us, G-d does not choose to reject any of us. We are the ones who turn our backs on Him; yet because He is such a forgiving and loving G-d, merciful when we make mistakes, we should never distance ourselves or turn our backs on a relative or a friend. There are countless verses about G-d's higher love, but here are just a few to whet your appetite:

> But You, my LORD, are a compassionate and gracious God, slow to anger, full of love and truth (Psalm 86:15).

> From afar *ADONAI* appeared to me. "Yes, I have loved you with an everlasting love. Therefore I have drawn you with lovingkindness" (Jeremiah 31:2).

And because He loved us so much, He made a way for us to spend eternity with Him by providing the perfect sacrifice, the unblemished Lamb of G-d, Yeshua.

> But God was rich in mercy, because of His great love with which He loved us. Even when we were dead in our trespasses, He made us alive together with Messiah. (By grace you have been saved!) (Ephesians 2:4–5).

The love of G-d is one of my favorite topics— but let's get back to the tribe talk.

In addition to being Jewish, my DNA also shows that I am 41 percent English. One day, I looked up my grandfather's English name "Carvel" to see if

147

there was any royalty in that lineage, and the name came up with the meaning, "swamp dweller." When I read that, any jewels I imagined on my crown became scratched, plastic rhinestones, so I'll take the royal tribe of Judah. It's a powerful blood line that flowed through Yeshua HaMashiach Himself.

Yeshua is referred to as the "Lion of the tribe of Judah" in Revelation 5:5. The setting is G-d's throne, as revealed to the Apostle John while he was exiled on the island of Patmos. According to John, surrounding the throne of G-d were twenty-four other thrones, and seated on them were twenty-four elders, dressed in white and with gold crowns on their head. "From the throne came flashes of lightning, rumblings and peals of thunder. In front of the throne, seven lamps were blazing" (Revelation 4:5, NIV)). According to the book of Revelation, those lamps were the seven spirits of G-d.

Then there was an image not unlike the image of the throne that Daniel spoke about in his prophetic book. Here is the Revelation account:

> In the middle of the throne and around it were four living creatures, full of eyes in front and behind. The first living creature was like a lion, the second living creature was like an ox, the third living creature had a face like a man, and the fourth living creature was like a flying eagle. The four living creatures, each having six wings, were full of eyes all around and within. They do not rest day or night, chanting,"Kadosh, kadosh, kadosh *ADONAI Elohei-Tzva'ot, asher haya v'hoveh v'yavo!* Holy, holy, holy is the LORD God of

Hosts, who was and who is and who is to come!" (Revelation 4:6–8).

Now compare this to how Daniel describes G-d's throne:

Daniel said: "I was looking in my vision at night, and behold, the four winds of heaven were churning up the great sea. Four huge beasts came up from the sea, each different from the others. The first was like a lion with eagle's wings. As I watched, its wings were pulled off and it was lifted off the ground. It was made to stand upon two feet like a man, and the heart of a human was given to it. "And behold there before me was another beast, a second one, like a bear. It raised itself up on one side; it had three ribs in its mouth between its teeth. It was told, 'Arise, devour much flesh!' After that I looked, and behold, there was another one like a leopard. On its back it had four wings like those of a bird. The beast also had four heads, and it was given authority to rule. After this in my vision at night, I looked and behold there was a fourth beast—terrifying, frightening, tremendously strong, with large iron teeth. It devoured and crushed—and anything that was left it trampled with its feet. It was different from all the beasts that came before it; it had ten horns (Daniel 7:2–7).

These passages are too similar to be a coincidence. The book of Daniel was written almost 700 years prior to John's writing of Revelation. In the midst of John's overwhelming visual of G-d's throne, there is a mighty angel asking the question, "Who is worthy to break the seal and open the scroll and break the seals?" (Revelation 5:2). The scroll referred to represents the plan for the end of time as we know it, the once-and-for all destruction of evil, and the entry of the New Jerusalem where believers will live in the presence of G-d forever.

And as it turned out, only Yeshua could open the seals. "Stop weeping! Behold, the Lion of the tribe of Judah, the Root of David, has triumphed—He is worthy to open the scroll and its seven seals" (Revelation 5:5).

Heady stuff. Judah is a tribe with some clout.

However, it's the patriarch Moses, from the tribe of Levi, who has made many repeat appearances in my life. If I had to choose a biblical personality closest to mine, it would be the demeanor of Moses—an excuse-maker, lacking confidence, bold (almost brazen) with G-d, and a runner.

When I first experienced a call to seminary in 2003, I was jazzed. I went to an informational meeting about the school; and before I knew it, I was having transcripts sent and recommendation letters written, and I was applying for financial aid. But then my feet turned cold. I was working full-time. I had small children. My husband was not in town during the week. *I don't know why I am doing this.* I began to back-pedal and made excuses, a lot like Moses did when *ADONAI* called him to "set the captives free."

During this stretch, I was in charge of an event to bring the well-known apologist Lee Strobel to town. It had been a great series of four sold-out events with Strobel. On the last day, I was supposed to take him and his wife Leslie to the airport, when my husband noticed my car was not in the driveway. He asked, "Where's your car?"

"In the driveway."

"No, it's not."

We realized our large, red SUV had been stolen. I knew if we had to replace this vehicle, we would not be able to afford a $600-per-month seminary payment. Four days passed, and our car had not shown up. Our insurance agent thought it was gone forever, so I began to make plans to defer seminary. I prayed, "If you want me to attend seminary, you will have to bring the car back, L-RD." The next morning, we received a call from the police department saying they'd found our vehicle after a high-speed chase with the thieves, and it was in perfect condition.

Then there was a scenario surrounding financial aid. I had typed my name differently on the seminary application than I had on the financial aid application. The two didn't jive, so I had no financial assistance. By that time, I really did not want to move forward, so I told G-d, "Well, I guess I'm not supposed to go to seminary." I literally prayed in the parking lot of my workplace, telling *ADONAI* I was going to defer for a year, and I asked for a miracle if He wanted me to attend. When I walked up to my office and turned on my computer, I had an email waiting for me from the Perkins School of Theology that said, "Congratulations, you have just received a 40 percent tuition-reduction grant."

After Moses and G-d worked through all of his excuses, he fulfilled his calling to lead the Israelites out of Egypt. He didn't look back, and neither did I, once I was certain seminary was a calling from *ADONAI.* In the dean of students' opening address to the new students, Moses made his appearance again. The dean said, "G-d didn't ask Moses to lead his people out of Egypt, then abandon him. No, G-d was with Moses every step of the way, guiding him with a pillar of cloud by day and a pillar of fire at night."

And that was true for me, all the way down to the L-RD's showing me which questions to study for a test and providing the verbiage for the numerous papers I was required to write.

I may not be from the tribe of Levi like Moses, but I guess if we go back far enough, we're all related.

Chapter 11
The Temple

There is something special about the Western Wall in Jerusalem. Perhaps it's because the Wall, known as the "Kotel" in Israel, was once the closest to the Holy of Holies where the Spirit of G-d resided, and also where the Ark of the Covenant was protected. Maybe it's significant because it's a reminder of the Jewish people's ongoing devotion to *ADONAI* throughout history.

Before I personally visited Israel, I told Facebook friends I wanted to pray for them at this special place. I asked them to send me their prayer requests in a private message, I would place them in the cracks of the Wall. Inserting prayers in the crevices of the Kotel is a longtime Jewish tradition that was revived during the Six Day War when Israeli soldiers took control of the Temple Mount and the Western Wall. Israeli Defense Minister Moshe Dayan was the first to reach the sacred site; he placed a written petition into one of the cracks, which was later revealed to be a prayer for a lasting peace to descend on the House of Israel.[xliv] Many of us still pray regularly for the peace of Jerusalem.

When I volunteered to insert my friends' requests in the openings of the Wall, I never dreamed I'd receive such an enthusiastic response. Their prayers flooded my Facebook Messenger account, and I remember writing out all of those needs on tiny slips of paper in my hotel room the night before my visit.

When I had my moment at the Western Wall in December 2014, men and women were separated along the expanse of the 160-foot-wide, 60-foot-tall edifice. That partially changed in January 2016, when the Israeli government approved the creation of an "egalitarian" prayer space where non-Orthodox Jewish men and women can pray together.[xlv]

In my December 2014 moment at the Western Wall, the men and women were still separated; and I remember that as I stood there at that historic site with other women, some had their prayer books in front of them quietly praying. Others swayed back and forth in deep meditation. I spent my time pressing the individual concerns into the crevices of the stones, knowing G-d saw my heart as I lifted up each friend by name. I felt His presence at that site.

I assumed with so many people doing exactly what I was doing, by the end of each day, those countless prayers would be gathered and destroyed. However, I was wrong. According to one source, Jewish law considers the little pieces of paper "holy" and dictates that holy texts may not be destroyed. So twice annually—before Passover in the springtime

154

and before the Jewish New Year in the fall—the notes are meticulously removed by workers who care for the site. The scraps of paper are then buried in a sacred cemetery on the Mount of Olives, treated with the same respect as damaged prayer books or Torah scrolls. Out of privacy, the notes are never read, and the slips of paper have never been counted.[xlvi]

Millions of people visit the Western Wall every year. As I studied King Solomon's building of the first Temple, I made another interesting discovery. The king who designed and constructed the Temple prophesied about a time in history when visitors, both Jewish and Gentiles, would gather at the Temple site to pray. You can find this prophetic word in 2 Chronicles:

> Moreover, concerning the foreigner who is not of Your people Israel but comes from a distant land for the sake of Your great Name and Your mighty hand and Your outstretched arm, when they come and pray toward this House, then may You hear from heaven, Your dwelling place and do whatever the foreigner asks of You. Then all the peoples of the earth will acknowledge Your Name and revere You, as Your people Israel do, and they will know that this House which I have built is called by Your Name (2 Chronicles 6:32–33).

It took Solomon seven years to construct the original Temple, fulfilling his father King David's wishes to provide a proper home for Almighty G-d. Online Jewish resource Chabad.org summarizes the effort it took to complete the Temple structure.

Tens of thousands of men were needed to perform the many tasks required for the gigantic undertaking. Men were sent to Lebanon to cut down cedar trees. Stones were hewn near the quarries, and then brought up to Moriah, there to be fitted together. In the valley of the Jordan the bronze was cast. Craftsmen were brought in from Tyre to help perfect the work. Ships set sail eastward and westward to bring the choicest materials for the adornment of the House of G-d. For the next 410 years, the Jewish people would bring daily offerings in this magnificent edifice, and here the nation would gather three times a year to "see and to be seen by the face of G-d." Here the Divine Presence was manifest. Ten daily miracles—such as the wind never extinguishing the fire on the altar—attested to G-d's presence in the Temple.[xlvii]

However, this holy Temple was destroyed during the Babylonian's siege of Jerusalem in 586 BC and not rebuilt until 515 BC after King Cyrus of Persia, who had conquered Babylon, allowed the Jewish people to return to Jerusalem and rebuild the Temple. Zerubbabel, who the prophet Haggai identifies as the head of Judea after the exile, steered the rebuilding project. Detailed in the book of Ezra, the Jewish people spent seven months getting settled in their homes, then began the undertaking with construction of the altar for sacrifices, segueing to laying the foundation. After some opposition from neighboring people groups, the building stopped temporarily. But after King Darius took over Persia, he issued a decree ordering that the building proceed again. He closed out the decree with this strong language:

156

"Furthermore, I decree that if anyone changes this edict, a beam is to be pulled out from his house, and let him be lifted up and impaled on it, and because of this, his house be made a pile of refuse. May God, who makes His name to dwell there, overthrow any king or people who lifts his hand to cause such change to destroy this House of God in Jerusalem. I Darius have issued a decree; let it be carried out with diligence" (Ezra 6:11–12).

So King Darius paved the way for the Temple to be completed. The second Temple had two courtyards, with the inner courtyard being 500 by 100 cubits (about 750 by 150 feet). There were most likely four gates in the wall of the outer courtyard, and at least one of them faced a street. There were probably two gates to the inner courtyard. Various chambers surrounded the Temple in both courtyards; however, most were in the outer courtyard and used for the storage of tithes, equipment, and vessels. The construction was completed in 515 BC.[xlviii]

Zerubbabel and his gang built the Temple, but they neglected to repair the walls around the city; and with no walls or gates, the city—and the Temple— were left vulnerable and exposed to their enemies. G-d recruited a Jewish man named Nehemiah, who still lived in Persia, to lead that aspect of the project. I love the story of Nehemiah because it contains so many lessons for us personally.

Nehemiah had not made the journey back to Israel because he had landed a job as the king's cupbearer; he knew he could be killed by walking out on the job or even asking for a leave of absence. The cupbearer was the head of security for the kingdom; and, yes, he put his life on the line, drinking out of the king's cup first to make sure the king wasn't slipped a lethal lemonade. Dropping everything to help his countrymen out would be a very unpopular thing to do and could cost him his life.

When Nehemiah heard the news about the state of Jerusalem, he sat down and cried; he was burdened for his people and couldn't do anything about it. He shared their vision of rebuilding the wall but felt helpless because he was locked into his job. For a number of days Nehemiah mourned, fasted, and prayed, and then he ended his quiet time with this: "Please, my LORD, let Your ear be attentive to the prayer of Your servant and to the prayer of Your servants who delight in revering Your Name. Give Your servant success today and grant compassion in the presence of this man" (Nehemiah 1:11).

"This man" was the king of Persia, Artaxerxes. So Nehemiah prayed up, fasted, gulped, and then entered into the presence of the king. Another part of Nehemiah's job as cupbearer was to always boost the mood of the king. He could never have a bad day in front of his majesty, because any display of his personal feelings could jeopardize his position. But for the first time ever, Nehemiah appeared before the king wearing a frown. The king asked him, "Why does your face look so sad when you are not ill? This can be nothing but sadness of heart."

Let's pause for a moment as Nehemiah turns to the audience and admits he is afraid. Not just a little afraid; he said he is very much afraid. So just in case the king didn't like his sour face and before he explained his unhappy demeanor, he threw in a little kingly praise: *May the king live forever!* Then he told his majesty what was going on, "Why should my face not be sad, when the city where my ancestors are buried lies in ruins, and its gates have been destroyed by fire?" (Nehemiah 2:3).

Off with his head!! No, that's not what happened. The king didn't react with rage. He asked Nehemiah what he wanted. I love this, because before Nehemiah responded, to make sure he answered the king in the way G-d wanted him to answer, he prayed again, right in the middle of this touchy conversation. Wow!

Have you ever done that? You'll be having a difficult chat with someone and you are praying silently all the way through it? "L-RD, I don't know what to say to her. Give me some words! I need clarity!" That is what Nehemiah did. He didn't want to utter a syllable the L-RD didn't bless. So after praying, he laid it out, "If it seems good to the king and if your servant has found favor in your sight, send me to the city in Judah where my ancestors are buried that I may rebuild it" (Nehemiah 2:5). Although the Word doesn't show it, I have to believe there was a long pause after this request. At that point, I am sure Nehemiah's head was bowed and he was prepared to die.

But remember, Nehemiah had a call from G-d to return to his homeland. He had prayed for favor with the king. He had petitioned G-d while in the middle of his conversation with his royal superior. We have to remember that when G-d calls us to take on a project, no matter what the obstacles are, He will clear the path to accomplish what He's called us to.

Meanwhile, back at the palace, the king, with the queen sitting stately beside him, asked "How long will your journey take, and when will you return?" (Verse 6). What? The king was letting him go? Maybe he should have kissed the king's hand and run out after that, but Nehemiah was feeling so good about the way things were going, he decided to push for a few more perks. He asked for letters from the governors of the areas he would pass through to get to Jerusalem so he'd have safe passage. Then, he pushed the royal privilege a little further, requesting some wood from the king's forest for the wall, the gates and for a little house he'd build while he was on temporary leave in Jerusalem. Why not go for it? The king agreed; but in reality, it was G-d who was faithful to provide.

Although Nehemiah experienced the privileges that came with being the king's cupbearer, it's safe to say G-d raised him up "for a time such as this." Through Nehemiah's leadership, the wall and gates of the city were rebuilt, despite opposition again from a couple of unfriendly neighbors named Sanballat the Horonite and Tobiah the Ammonite. When they cooked up a scheme to pull Nehemiah away from the project so they could eliminate him, he sent a message that would later become a somewhat famous and oft-repeated verse. He said to tell them, "I am doing an important work, so I cannot come down."

Nehemiah believed in what he was doing, just as I believe in this book.

Anytime we want to motivate people, we have to show them our own enthusiasm about the project. We must be confident about what we are doing so others will believe in it too.

Leadership author and speaker John Maxwell says people need to see your conviction. He tells the story about Scottish philosopher and religious skeptic David Hume, who was observed hurrying early one morning to hear evangelist George Whitefield preach. When someone asked where he was going and was told, "To hear George Whitefield," the questioner asked him if he believed what the evangelist preached. "Certainly not!" Hume replied, "But Whitefield does, and I want to hear a man who does." To get others to follow, people need to see our conviction.[xlix]

So *ADONAI* began the process of restoration with Judah, and His people started out with the right attitude. They understood why they were allowed to be carried off into exile. They comprehended that they had not been obedient to G-d and had followed other gods. To help the people start off fully knowledgeable about the dos and don'ts in G-d's world, Ezra the scribe stood on a lofty wooden platform and began to praise G-d before reading the Words of the law. The people praised G-d along with him, bowing down and worshipping the L-RD with their faces to the ground.

Conviction pelted the Israelites like a heavy rain storm, and they were drenched in their tears. But I love this. When Nehemiah witnessed their remorse, he said, "Do not grieve, for the joy of *ADONAI* is your strength" (Nehemiah 8:10). That's another wonderful verse to claim when life is a little more difficult than you'd like. *Do not grieve, for the joy of ADONAI is your strength.*

The Jewish people, my people, rededicated their lives to G-d. I know how they felt. When you look back and see all the wasted years, all the years you could have been following G-d and His Son, Yeshua, but didn't, it's heart wrenching, and there is a sense of loss.

But there is also joy in finally discovering the truth and completing a G-d-inspired project like the Temple. There was a party of great magnitude to celebrate the rebuilding of the second Temple. The dedication included songs of thanksgiving, with the music of cymbals, harps, and lyres. There were two large choirs on top of the walls to give thanks. And on that day, they offered great sacrifices, because G-d had given them supernatural joy. Nehemiah 12:43 says "The joy in Jerusalem could be heard from far off."

What a spectacular day! Little did the celebrants know that in 70 AD the Romans would make a run on Jerusalem and the Temple, all except a portion of the Western Wall, would come tumbling down again.

But here's the good news. The Word of G-d prophesies that there will be a third and a fourth Temple. In Daniel 12, Daniel speaks about the "end of days" when there will once again be daily sacrifices made in a third Temple.

162

The plans for a third Temple are in place. When in Israel, I toured the Temple Institute Museum, where many of the contents of the next Temple are "move-in ready" for the structure once it's built.

The Temple Institute and the Temple Mount and Eretz Yisrael Faithful Movement are the two main Jewish organizations responsible for making preparations for the third Temple and the reinstatement of sacrificial worship. According to the Temple Institute, other organizations have plans as well. One wants to pitch a tabernacle-style tent on the Mount; another wants to build a synagogue in one of the corners of the platform.

The director of the Temple Institute, Chaim Richman, believes "Buildings don't fall down from heaven." He adds, "It's a mitzvah to build the Temple," citing Exodus 25:8, and says that Jews should be performing all 613 mitzvot, which requires a Temple. He also says that the third Temple will "bring the Light back into the world" that left the Temple Mount when the L-RD's divine presence departed.[1]

The founder of the Temple Institute is Rabbi Yisrael Ariel, who served in the paratrooper brigade that liberated the Temple Mount in the Six Day War of 1967, and he was one of the first soldiers to reach the Mount. Rabbi Ariel was the Rosh Yeshiva and spiritual leader of the city of Yamit in the Sinai, which was dismantled as part of the peace accords with Egypt. He is a scholar and author of many Hebrew works, including *Atlas of the Biblical Boundaries of the Land of Israel.*[li]

Rabbi Ariel clearly demonstrates in his writings the belief and conviction, as emphasized by Torah scholars and luminaries of earlier generations and supported by his extensive Torah knowledge and wisdom, that every generation is obligated to do all within its power toward rebuilding the holy Temple.

The Temple Institute has begun to restore and construct the sacred vessels for the service of the holy Temple. They are made according to the exact specifications of the Bible and have been constructed from the original source materials, such as gold, copper, silver, and wood. These are authentic, accurate vessels, not merely replicas or models. All of these items are fit and ready for use in the service of the holy Temple. Among the many items featured in the exhibition are musical instruments played by the Levitical choir, the golden crown of the High Priest, and gold and silver vessels used in the incense and sacrificial services. After many years of effort and toil, the Institute has completed the three most important and central vessels of the divine service: the seven-branched candelabra, or Menorah, made of pure gold; the golden incense altar; and the golden table of the showbread. Other completed projects include the sacred uniform of the Kohein Gadol, the High Priest. This project was the culmination of years of study and research. The High Priest's *Choshen* (Breastplate), *Ephod*, and the *tzitz* (a platelet of gold worn on the forehead) have been completed.[lii]

However, according to Daniel 12:11, those sacrifices will be abolished when the "abomination of desolation" occurs during a seven-day tribulation period. What is an abomination of desolation? It will be a time when idolatrous or inappropriate sacrifices will be made at the Temple. The holy Temple will be compromised.

In an article written by Tom Clark, a charismatic pastor who has served congregations all over the world, he says, "The Hebrew root for abomination is *shaqats*, which means 'to be filthy,' 'to loath,' 'to abhor'" ('Abomination of Desolation,' *International Standard Bible Encyclopedia*). It is most often used to describe idolatrous worship practices, especially those most offensive to a sense of decency and morality. The New Testament equivalent means "detestable." Albert Barnes adds that the phrase *the abomination of desolation* "is a Hebrew expression meaning an abominable or hateful destroyer."[liii]

Yeshua speaks about this same abomination in Matthew 24, and says when it happens it is a sign of terrible things to come.

> So when you see standing in the holy place "the abomination that causes desolation," spoken of through the prophet Daniel—let the reader understand—then let those who are in Judea flee to the mountains. Let no one on the housetop go down to take anything out of the house. Let no one in the field go back to get their cloak. How dreadful it will be in those days for pregnant women and nursing mothers! Pray that your flight will not take place in winter or on the Sabbath. For then there will be great distress, unequaled from the beginning of the world until now—and never to be equaled again. "If those

days had not been cut short, no one would survive, but for the sake of the elect those days will be shortened. At that time if anyone says to you, "Look, here is the Messiah!" or, "There he is!" do not believe it. For false messiahs and false prophets will appear and perform great signs and wonders to deceive, if possible, even the elect. See, I have told you ahead of time (Matthew 24:15–25).

And after this stretch of time, a seven-year period of tribulation, Yeshua will return again and reign on earth for a thousand years. Those who now believe in Yeshua will have already been raptured to heaven and will avoid this time of woe (in my opinion, though the timing of the rapture is controversial). In 1 Thessalonians 4:16–17 it says, "For the LORD Himself will come down from heaven, with a loud command, with the voice of the archangel and with the trumpet call of G-d, and the dead in Christ will rise first. After that, we who are still alive and are left will be caught up together with them in the clouds to meet the LORD in the air."

I have had two vivid dreams about Yeshua's return, one when I was sixteen and the other more recently. When I was a teenager, I clearly heard the shofar sound and met Yeshua in the air. I woke up saying the name "Jesus" aloud. I had been reading in the book of Revelation, but I think I was too young to handle such a powerful dream. It scared me so much that I didn't study Revelation for many years after that.

My second dream was more recent. I appeared to be sleeping in a stark nursing-care facility when the shofar sounded again. While the surroundings were depressing, what occurred upon the Messiah's return was not. This time I flew out of my bed, my garments changed to white, and then I permeated a brick wall and met Yeshua in the air. This glorious day will be the future of all who believe in Yeshua as Savior and Messiah.

Just before the Son of G-d comes back again for a millennial reign on earth, Matthew 24 says the sun and moon will go dark, the stars will fall from the sky, and the heavens will be shaken. These supernatural events remind me a little of what happened after Yeshua was crucified. In Matthew 27 it says the curtain of the Temple was torn in two from top to bottom. The earth shook, the rocks split, and the tombs broke open. People who had long been dead came out of their graves and walked into Jerusalem and appeared to many people.

One Roman centurion, probably guarding the crucifixion site, said, "Surely He was the Son of God!" (Matthew 27:54, NIV).

Once the whole world loses power, the light of the world, Yeshua, will make His grand and glorious entrance. At that point, everyone from across the world will see Him, and mourn because they didn't get it the first time.

There will also be a loud blast of a trumpet or shofar, and countless angels will join Yeshua. It will be a spectacular day—the beginning of Yeshua's one-thousand-year reign on earth.

It's during this reign that a fourth and final Temple will emerge, referred to as the Millennial

Temple and prophesied about in detail in Ezekiel 40-48.

According to Zechariah 6:12–13, Yeshua will actually build the Temple and will rule there. Ezekiel 40:2 tells us the Temple will not be situated where the current Temple Mount is located. Instead it will be set on a very high mountain to the north of Jerusalem, suggesting that the topography of Jerusalem and the surrounding area could be transformed upon Yeshua's return. The fourth Temple will be walled and guarded and will be decorated with palm trees throughout, and carved cherubim will be in the most holy place, the inner sanctuary.

A palm tree has great significance, as it represents victory. When Yeshua entered Jerusalem on a lowly donkey before His crucifixion, His followers laid down palm branches in front of Him, suggesting the victorious king had entered the city; however, at that time, He was not the type of warrior king they desired, one that might overthrow the oppressive Roman rule. This go around, Yeshua will return as a conquering King, defeating death, principalities, and false beliefs.

The palm tree is mentioned numerous times in the Bible, but one particular passage about a palm tree, in Psalm 92:13–14, changed my life forever. It reads: "The righteous will flourish like a palm tree. He will grow like a cedar in Lebanon. Planted in the House of *ADONAI*, they will flourish in the courts of our God."

Palm trees live for about 800 years, cedars of Lebanon over a thousand. This passage says they really flourish when planted in the House of the L-RD; and if the righteous plant themselves in the courts of G-d, they'll flourish as well. This verse came alive to me one day, and it radically changed my prayer life. While I had spent a lot of time in the word of G-d, my prayers were short, general, and not too personal. I decided that in order to flourish, I needed to spend more prayer time with ADONAI in His court, lifting up every need in my life as well as the needs of those I care about. I began to see breakthrough in many areas through this extended stay in G-d's presence, and the palm tree once again represented "victory."

The Millennial Temple will be guarded by priests, the sons of Zadok. As you may remember, the sons of Zadok were the only priests who did not betray King David when David's biological sons, first Absalom and then later Adonijah, staged separate revolts to take over David's kingdom.

In the fourth Temple there will once again be sacrifices: grain, sin, and guilt offerings (Ezekiel 40:41). So why, if we believe that Yeshua was the one true sacrifice for eternity, would there be sacrifices offered in the Temple again? According to my friend and author, Jeanne Nigro, who teaches about the Millennial Temple, we have misunderstood the original sacrifices performed in the earlier temples. In an interview she did with author and television host David Reagan, founder of Lamb & Lion Ministries, she said, "I believe we have to go back to Leviticus to understand why there were sacrifices in the Temple, and we have to understand that temple sacrifices had a completely different purpose then Yeshua's sacrifice. Never were temple sacrifices to do with eternal life or to remove sin. They were more about physically going into G-d's manifest presence in the Temple and not burning up."[liv]

When people bring their offerings into the fourth Temple, they will leave in the opposite way they came, proving once again that G-d is a G-d of order. A favorite passage of mine concerning *ADONAI's* order is found in Proverbs: "Trust in *ADONAI* with all your heart, lean not on your own understanding. In all your ways acknowledge Him, and He will make your paths straight" (Proverbs 3:5-6).

In the article, "The Temple of Ezekiel," author Lambert Dolphin says there will be similarities to the first two Temples constructed, but there will be the following differences:

- No wall of partition to exclude Gentiles
- No Court of Women
- No laver (Ezekiel 36:24–27)
- No table of shewbread (Micah 5:4; John 6:35)
- No lampstand or Menorah (Isaiah 49:6; John 8:12)
- No golden altar of incense (Zechariah 8:20–23; John 14:6)
- No veil (Isaiah 25:6–8; Mathew 27:51)
- No Ark of the Covenant (Jeremiah 3:16; John 10:30-33)[lv]

Once the Temple is in place, Ezekiel 43:2 says the glory of the G-d of Israel will come from the east, with a "voice like the roar of rushing waters." The east gate that the L-RD enters through will remain shut, since He came through that gate. The land will be radiant with His glory; and according to Ezekiel 43:5, the glory of ADONAI will fill the Temple. When Ezekiel received an eye-full of what was going to happen, he could do nothing but fall flat on his face in reverence.

The Temple will also be the site of Yeshua's throne, and we will worship Him in His presence as He lives among His people forever.

There is something addictive about being in the L-RD's presence. I remember one event where I was speaking. I arrived early, and while the worship band was rehearsing, they placed me in a back room to pray and to go over my message. However, the music ushered in the presence of G-d (Psalm 100:4) and it seeped into the back room where I was sitting. It was intoxicating. I couldn't concentrate on my message. Think about the moments when you felt closest to *ADONAI*, and multiply it times a thousand. I think we will be so overwhelmed by *ADONAI*'s presence that we will react like Ezekiel and fall prostrate to the ground.

For those of us water lovers, there will actually be a river running through the Millennial Temple; and it will flow as far as the Dead Sea, where the water will become fresh again, like it once was in Eden. I remember my visit to the Dead Sea where, because of the salt content, I floated without a raft. It was a

171

cool phenomenon, but it was also sad because there was nothing living in that body of water.

The Dead Sea's life was snuffed out during the time of the patriarch Abraham, due to the sin of Sodom and Gomorrah. Abraham and his nephew Lot separated ways because their respective people were quarreling, and their possessions were becoming too great for the land to handle. Abraham gave Lot his choice of areas. Lot looked around and saw that the "whole plain of the Jordan toward Zoar was well watered, like the Garden of the L-RD, like the land of Egypt" (Genesis 13:10, NIV) and that is the area he decided to settle in, the region near the Dead Sea and Sodom and Gomorrah.

But the people of that land committed what the L-RD called grievous sin, and G-d decided to wipe out Sodom and Gomorrah. In His mercy, *ADONAI* saved the only righteous inhabitants, Lot and his family, before He destroyed the two cities with burning sulfur. One stipulation as Lot and his family members fled the fiery inferno they once called home was that they were not to look back, or they would die like the rest of their neighbors. Curiosity got the best of Lot's wife. She took a deadly peek and because of that, she turned into a pillar of salt. It's interesting that the Dead Sea is composed of mostly salt and minerals.

So G-d will restore the Dead Sea to its previous, fruitful state. In Zechariah 14:8 (NIV), it says, "On that day living water will flow out from Jerusalem, half of it east to the Dead Sea and half of it west to the Mediterranean Sea." Ezekiel 47:8-10 claims that when the living water from the fourth Temple empties into the Dead Sea, the salty water there will become fresh, and swarms of living creatures will live there, "large numbers of fish," and there will once again be fishermen on its banks, where fruit trees will grow again.

It's a reminder that only G-d can bring the dead back to life, as He did with His only Son, Yeshua, and as He plans to do with our bodies one day. In Romans 8:10–11, the apostle Paul explains, "But if Messiah is in you, though the body is dead because of sin, yet the Spirit is alive because of righteousness. And if the *Ruach* of the One who raised *Yeshua* from the dead dwells in you, the One who raised Messiah *Yeshua* from the dead will also give life to your mortal bodies through His *Ruach* who dwells in you."

And there is great news for those who are tired of the fighting along the Gaza Strip or the threat of missiles being fired into Israel. After a long fight over the land that G-d first gave to the Israelites, it will finally belong to the Jews and will be divided up amongst the twelve tribes. With Yeshua and the Spirit of the L-RD living with His people again, the city where the Temple is located will also be renamed: "*ADONAI* is there" (Ezekiel 48:35).

Gentiles and Jews alike need to realize that this one-thousand-year reign of Yeshua will look very "Jewish," so we must ask, "What are we doing to educate ourselves? Are we going to be ready? Will we recognize Yeshua when He plants His feet on the Mount of Olives prior to His millennial reign?

Chapter 12
True Shalom

As I obediently type the final words of this book, the world is attempting to emerge from a global pandemic, "COVID-19." The Coronavirus shut down life as we know it—closing synagogues and churches, businesses, and stores. Everyone has been affected in some way, and at this time in history, we need G-d's shalom—his peace—more than ever.

The word "shalom" has more packed into its Hebrew meaning than meets the eye. Shalom can be defined as "wholeness, completeness, soundness, health, safety, and prosperity, carrying with it the implication of permanence."[lvi]

However, I've found that peace cannot be obtained by a snap of the fingers. We cannot wish shalom on ourselves or call it forth in our own power. It is supernatural and it's something that Yeshua promises those who believe in Him. In Psalm 122:6, King David himself said we have to pray for peace, and he encouraged us to pray for the peace of

Jerusalem. Then he said, "May those who love you be at peace!"

While I love Jerusalem and Israel, I am prone to anxiety; at one time I suffered a couple of panic attacks when I was trying to juggle post-graduate work, a full-time job, and a young family while my husband Jeff was out-of-town during the week. At that time, Jeff and I knew I was called to seminary, so we took the plunge and I left my full-time job.

After reducing my schedule, the panic attacks stopped, but I can still feel anxious at times. COVID-19 has triggered some tense feelings in my spirit, especially first thing in the morning when I wake up. For a while, we were sheltering at home, and there was no place to go, no events to attend, no dinners out, and no speaking engagements on the calendar. I have always enjoyed my freedom, and I felt like a caged lion in my home, looking for a means of escape.

I've found there's only one way to calm the beastly, anxious feelings. Once I've made my coffee, I enter G-d's presence by praising Him, then I read His Word and pray. That is when Yeshua's inexplicable peace envelops me, and the anxiety disappears. Philippians 4:6–7 says, "Do not be anxious about anything—but in everything, by prayer and petition with thanksgiving, let your requests be made known to G-d. And the shalom of G-d, which surpasses all understanding, will guard your hearts and your minds in Messiah Yeshua."

The Greek word "guard" here means "to prevent a hostile invasion."[lvii] Anxiety is not of G-d, and it will take us over if we don't press into *ADONAI's* shalom, especially as the days ahead are promised to be increasingly more difficult.

Yeshua is prophesied as Sar Shalom, the "Prince of Peace" in Isaiah 9: "For unto us a child is born, unto us a son is given, and the government will be upon His shoulders. And He will be called Wonderful Counselor, Mighty G-d, Everlasting Father, Prince of Peace. Of the increase of His government and peace there will be no end. He will reign on David's throne and over His kingdom, establishing and upholding it with justice and righteousness from that time and forever" (Isaiah 9:6–7, NIV).

In John 14:27, Yeshua fulfills this prophesy when He says, "Peace I leave with you; my peace I give you. I do not give to you as the world gives. Do not let your hearts be troubled and do not be afraid." The Greek word for peace here is very similar to "shalom" and means "peace, harmony, tranquility, safety, welfare and health."[lviii]

Even without a pandemic going on, life is tough. Yeshua reminded us of that in John 16:33 when He said, "These things I have spoken to you, so that in Me you may have *shalom*. In the world you will have trouble, but take heart! I have overcome the world!"

Colossians 3:15 says that through faith in Yeshua, it is possible for peace to rule in our hearts, not fear or worry.

I am not sure where I'd be without the shalom of *ADONAI* in my life.

What about you? Have you been wandering, looking for peace and meaning in your life?

In one of the flower beds in my front yard, I have some ground cover called "Wandering Jew" that is supposed to fill up the open spots on the ground. The name "Wandering Jew" is not a flattering term. It originated in medieval folklore and referred to a Jew condemned to wander the earth restlessly until the second coming of Christ because of his scornful attitude just before the crucifixion.[lix]

However, my "Wandering Jew" is not wandering anymore like it used to, so I thought it represented a great analogy of how this wandering Jew is not wandering either—I am no longer searching for identity and confirmation that my Jewish roots mean something. I believe *ADONAI* now plans to use them for His glory, prior to the ultimate glory that we will see once all things are restored.

So if you are wandering, here's some hope. One day, as Zechariah 14:4 (NIV) prophesies, Yeshua will return to the same place where He ascended from over two thousand years ago, the Mount of Olives. "On that day His feet will stand on the Mount of Olives, east of Jerusalem, and the Mount of Olives will be split in two from east to west, forming a great valley, with half of the mountain moving north and half moving south." It's prophesied that prior to this, the chosen ones will say the same words as they did when Yeshua made His final entry into Jerusalem before He was crucified: "Baruch haba b'shem *ADONAI!* This means "Blessed is He who comes in the name of the L-RD!"

178

But this does not happen until after a time of great distress when the enemy nations around Israel rise up against Jerusalem, and the city will be captured. However, that is when the L-RD will wage war against those nations and Yeshua will return as a conquering King.

Zechariah 14 goes on to describe this day of Yeshua's magnificent arrival: "On that day there will be neither sunlight nor cold, frosty darkness. It will be a unique day—a day known only to the L-RD— with no distinction between day and night. When evening comes, there will be light. On that day living water will flow out from Jerusalem, half of it east to the Dead Sea and half of it west to the Mediterranean Sea, in summer and in winter. The LORD will be king over the whole earth. On that day there will be one LORD, and His name the only name" (Zechariah 14:6–9). It is promised that Jerusalem will never again be destroyed, and that has to create a sense of peace in the soul. The survivors from the nations that attacked Jerusalem will make an about-face and will recognize Yeshua as L-RD and King and will celebrate the Festival of Tabernacles.

That will be a glorious day, but there will be an even more reigning peace than this when we as believers will all reside in what is referred as the "New Jerusalem."

At the end of time as we know it, according to Revelation 21:2 (NIV), this new Jerusalem will "come down from heaven from G-d, prepared as a bride beautifully dressed for her husband." Eden will be restored as G-d Himself will once again dwell with

His people. Revelation 21:4 (NIV) says "He will wipe every tear from their eyes. There will be no more death or mourning or crying or pain, for the old order of things has passed away." I don't know about you but I can't wait for that day. I know that I have probably shed enough tears over my lifetime to fill up an Olympic-sized pool. The idea that death will be defeated, and there will be no more mourning or pain is like someone just told me I have received a lifetime supply of my favorite chocolate chip cookies. This news elates me!

But there's one catch. We must believe in Yeshua and strive to be like Him in order to achieve the promised intimacy with Almighty G-d. It's a belief that gives us access to become part of G-d's family. 1 John 3:1–2 says, "See how glorious a love the Father has given us, that we should be called G-d's children—and so we are! The reason the world does not know us is that it did not know Him. Loved ones, now we are G-d's children; and it has not yet been revealed what we will be. But we do know that when it's revealed, we shall be like Him, because we will see Him just as He is. "

But Revelation 21:8 issues a stern warning: "But for the cowardly and faithless and detestable and murderers and sexually immoral and sorcerers and idolaters and all liars—their lot is in the lake that burns with fire and brimstone, which is the second death." It sounds a lot like what happened to Sodom and Gomorrah, and no one wants to end up in a salt shaker.

And according to the book of Revelation, the New Jerusalem will be a beautiful sight. It will be in the shape of a square with walls of jasper and streets of gold. The foundation of the city will be decorated with precious stones. The twelve gates, representing the twelve tribes of Israel will each be made of a single pearl. There will be no temple needed because the L-RD G-d Almighty and the Lamb of G-d, Yeshua, will be its Temple.

There also won't be any need for the sun or the moon anymore because the glory of *ADONAI* will give it light, and Yeshua will be its lamp. I can't wait! What about you?

Isaiah 11:6–8 (NIV) says wild animals will become like pets in the New Jerusalem. All of the cuddly stuffed animals we had as a child come to life and will be just as harmless. "The wolf will live with the lamb, the leopard will lie down with the goat, the calf and the lion and the yearling together; and a little child will lead them. The cow will feed with the bear, their young will lie down together, and the lion will eat straw like the ox. The infant will play near the cobra's den, and the young child will put its hand into the viper's nest."

Toward the end of the last chapter of Revelation, Yeshua describes Himself as the "Root and the Offspring of David, and the bright Morning Star." There is also an invitation from the Holy Spirit and the bride that says, "'Come! Let the one who is thirsty come and let the one who wishes take the free gift of the water of life" (Revelation 22:17, NIV).

Will you accept the invitation?

If so, here is a simple prayer you can pray to be assured of salvation and to reserve your place in the city of true shalom, the New Jerusalem.

Yeshua, I now believe that You are the promised Messiah of our people, and I thank You for Your sacrifice on the cross for my sin so that I can live eternally with You one day. I repent of my past wrongdoing and give my life to You today. Help me to know You and Your ways more intimately. I pray this in the name of Yeshua, AMEN.

If you prayed this prayer, welcome to the family; and be assured, it looks *very* Jewish.

About the Author

Lisa Burkhardt Worley is the nine-time award-winning author of ten books and a Bible study. She is the founder of Pearls of Promise Ministries (pearlsofpromiseministries.com) and is the Executive Producer and Co-host of the television and radio show, *POP Talk*, found on the Faith Unveiled Network, King Television Network, and the Fishbowl Radio Network. Burkhardt Worley serves as Intercessory Prayer Leader for Jewish Ministries at Gateway Church in Southlake, Texas, and is also the Vice-President of Marketing for international organization, Christian Women in Media. She earned a Masters of Theological Studies degree from SMU Perkins School of Theology, graduating Magna Cum Laude, and is working on her Doctor of Ministry with a concentration in Messianic Studies at The King's University.

Glossary of Terms

"*ADONAI*"– L-RD

"*ADONAI* Tzva'ot"– L-RD of Hosts

"*Angel of the L-RD*"– Christophany, or a pre-incarnate appearance of Jesus Christ

"*Ben Elohim*" – Sons of the G-ds

"*Dreidel*" – A spinning top with four sides featuring a different Hebrew letter. Used for a children's game at Hanukkah.

"*Hashkiveinu*" – A prayer traditionally recited in the evening, envisioning G-d as a guide and shelter.

"*Hineni*" – Here I am

"*Kedoshim*" – Holy ones

"*Kohamin*" – a member of the priestly class, having certain rights and duties in the synagogue

"*Mitzvot*"– Commandment

"*Olam ha-ba*" – The world to come

"*Olam ha-zeh*" – This world

"*Pesach*" – Passover

"*Ruach*" – Breath, Wind, Spirit

185

"*Ruach Elohim*" – The Spirit of G-d

"*Shofar*" – a ram's-horn trumpet used by ancient Jews in religious ceremonies and as a battle signal, now sounded at Rosh Hashanah and Yom Kippur.

"*Tanakh*"– Jewish Sacred Writings

'*Toda*" – Thanks

"*Torah*"– The law of G-d as revealed to Moses

"*Tzedakah*" – Blue and white tin box for the deposit of coins for charity

"*YHWH*" – A tetragrammaton made up of four Hebrew letters representing the biblical name for G-d.

Endnotes

---

[i] "How wide and deep was the Jordan River where Israel crossed?" Never Thirsty, https://www.neverthirsty.org/bible-qa/qa-archives/question/wide-deep-jordan-river-israel-crossed/ (Accessed June 18, 2020).

[ii] https://www.jewishvirtuallibrary.org/chicago-2

[iii] Jay Pridmore, "Exploring the Adler," https://www.chicagotribune.com/news/ct-xpm-1991-09-20-9103110447-story.html (Accessed June 22, 2020)

[iv] "Who is a Jew? Matrilineal Descent," My Jewish Learning, www.myjewishlearning.com/article/ask-the-epert-matrilineal-descent/ (Accessed April 15, 2020).

[v] "How Does Reform Judaism Define Who is a Jew?" ReformJudaism.org,

https://reformjudaism.org/practice/ask-rabbi/how-does-reform-judaism-define-who-jew
(Accessed April 15, 2020)

vi Ibid.

vii "Jewish Athletes —Marty Glickman and Sam Stoller, United States Holocaust Memorial Museum, https://www.ushmm.org/exhibition/olympics/?content=jewish_athletes_more (accessed June 22, 2020).

viii Aiden Pink, "New Rochelle Jewish Community Caught Inside Coronavirus 'Containment Zone,'" https://forward.com/news/breaking-news/441304/coronavirus-containment-zone-new-rochelle-new-york/ (Accessed April 17, 2020).

ix "The Shema," My Jewish Learning, https://www.myjewishlearning.com/article/the-shema/ (Accessed April 17, 2020).

x Jack W. Hayford, *NKJV Spirit-Filled Life Bible,* (Nashville: Thomas Nelson, 2018), 1505.

xi "What Does 'L-RD of Hosts Mean?'" One for Israel, https://www.oneforisrael.org/bible-based-teaching-from-israel/what-does-L-RD-of-hosts-mean/ (Accessed April 22, 2020).

xii "Reconstructing the Destruction of the Tabernacle of Shiloh," Jewish Bible Quarterly, https://jbqnew.jewishbible.org/jbq-past-issues/2016/441-january-march-2016/reconstructing-destruction-tabernacle-shiloh/ (Accessed April 22, 2020).

xiii "Moshe Kempinski – It's Time to Talk," CFOIC Heartland, https://www.cfoic.com/meet-israeli-pioneers/moshe-kempinski/ (Accessed April 23, 2020)

xiv "'To the Jew First': What Does it Mean and Why Does it Matter," One for Israel, https://www.oneforisrael.org/bible-based-teaching-from-israel/to-the-jew-first-what-does-it-mean-and-why-does-it-matter/ (accessed June 22, 2020).

xv The Jewish Annotated New Testament (New York, Oxford University Press, 2011), p.464.

xvi Ibid. Pg. 465

xvii Rabbi Jack Zimmerman, "Sukkot, The Feast of Booths (Known to some as the Feast of Tabernacles), https://www.jewishvoice.org/read/blog/sukkot-the-feast-of-booths-known-to-some-as-the-feast-of-tabernacles (Accessed April 28, 2020)

xviii John MacArthur, *The MacArthur Bible Commentary,* (Nashville: Thomas Nelson, 2005), 185.

xix Glen Scrivener, "Where is Jesus in the Old Testamet," https://www.desiringgod.org/articles/where-is-jesus-in-the-old-testament (accessed May 4, 2020).

xx Ibid.

xxi Carissa Quinn, "Who is the Angel of the L-RD?" https://bibleproject.com/blog/who-is-the-angel-of-the-L-RD/ (accessed May 5, 2020).

xxii Sheri Bell, "Did Jesus Fulfill Old Testament Prophecy?" https://www.josh.org/jesus-fulfill-prophecy/?mwm_id=241874010215&mot=J79GNF&gclid=EAIaIQobChMIqKvm-7qW6gIVC77ACh16qwqfEAAYASAAEgKnV_D_BwE (accessed May 5, 2020)

xxiii Andre LeMaire, "The Many Faces of King David," https://www.myjewishlearning.com/article/king-david/ (accessed May 6, 2020)

xxiv Dr. C. Truman Davis, "A Physician' View of the Crucifixion of Jesus Christ," https://www1.cbn.com/medical-view-of-the-crucifixion-of-jesus-christ (accessed May 7, 2020).

xxv "How Did Peter Die?" https://www.biblestudy.org/question/peter-die.html

(accessed May 11, 2020).

xxvi "Josephus'Account of Jesus: The Testimonium Flavianum," *Jewish Antiquities, 18.3.3 §63,* http://www.josephus.org/testimonium.htm (accessed May 12, 2020).

xxvii Shawn Aster, "The Twelve Minor Prophets," https://www.myjewishlearning.com/article/the-12-minor-prophets/ (accessed May 12, 2020)

xxviii Jacob Isaacs, "Isaiah the Prophet," https://www.chabad.org/library/article_cdo/aid/464019/jewish/Isaiah-The-Prophet.htm (accessed May 13, 2020).

xxix Dr. Eitan Bar, "Isaiah 53 – The Forbidden Chapter," https://www.oneforisrael.org/bible-based-teaching-from-israel/inescapable-truth-isaiah-53/ (accessed May 13, 2020).

xxx Bob Hostetler and Josh McDowell, "If I Had Faked the Resurrection," https://www.focusonthefamily.com/faith/if-i-had-faked-the-resurrection/ (accessed May 13, 2020).

xxxi Ibid.

xxxii Ibid.

xxxiii Jack W. Hayford, *NKJV Spirit-Filled Life Bible,* (Nashville: Thomas Nelson, 2018), 970.

xxxiv "Isaiah 53:10," Barnes Notes on the Bible, https://biblehub.com/commentaries/isaiah/53-10.htm (Accessed May 14, 2020).

xxxv Conrad Hackett and David McClendon, "Christians remain World's Largest Religious Group, but They are Declining in Europe," https://www.pewresearch.org/fact-tank/2017/04/05/christians-remain-worlds-largest-religious-group-but-they-are-declining-in-europe/ (accessed May 14, 2020).

xxxvi E. Ray Clendenen and Jeremy Royal Howard, *Holman Illustrated Bible Commentary,* (Nashville: B&H Publishing Group, 2015), 763.

xxxvii "Justify," Meriam-Webster, https://www.merriam-webster.com/dictionary/justify (accessed May 14, 2020).

xxxviii Don Finto, *The Handbook for the End Times,* (Bloomington: Chosen Books, 2018), 63.

xxxix Jack Wellman, "Romans 11: Bible Study, Commentary and Summary," https://www.patheos.com/blogs/christiancrier/201

6/05/26/romans-11-bible-study-commentary-and-summary/ (accessed May 15, 2020).

xl "Messianic Jews," Jewish Voice, https://www.jewishvoice.org/learn/messianic-jews (accessed May 15, 2020).

xli Ingrid Anderson, "Why the History of Messianic Judaism is so Fraught and Complicated," https://theconversation.com/why-the-history-of-messianic-judaism-is-so-fraught-and-complicated-106143 (accessed May 15, 2020).

xlii "Replacement Theology," ICEJ, https://int.icej.org/media/replacement-theology (accessed May 18, 2020).

xliii Robert Friedman, "Circumcision of the Heart," https://jewsforjesus.org/publications/issues/issues-v01-n06/circumcision-of-the-heart/, (accessed May 18, 2020)

xliv "The Western Wall, History & Overview," Jewish Virtual Library, https://www.jewishvirtuallibrary.org/history-and-overivew-of-the-western-wall, (Accessed May 18, 2020).

xlv Ibid.

xlvi "What Happens to Prayers at the Western Wall?" Sojourner, https://www.inspirationcruises.com/-/blog/2016/02/16/what-happens-to-prayer-notes-at-the-western-wall/, (accessed May 18, 2020).

xlvii "The Destruction of the First Holy Temple," Chabad.org, https://www.chabad.org/library/article_cdo/aid/144569/jewish/The-First-Temple.htm, (Accessed May 18, 2020).

xlviii Lawrence H. Schiffman, "Building the Second Temple," https://www.myjewishlearning.com/article/second-temple/, (accessed May 19, 2020).

xlix John Maxwell, "The Power of Good Communication," https://www.johnmaxwell.com/blog/the-power-of-good-communication/ (accessed May 20, 2020).

l "End-Tine Prophecy: Why is the Third Temple So Important?" The Messianic Prophecy Bible Project, https://free.messianicbible.com/feature/end-time-prophecy-why-is-the-third-temple-so-important/, (accessed May 21, 2020).

[li] Ofra Lax, "Ariel's Jerusalem: An Interview with Rabbi Yisrael Ariel," http://www.israelnationalnews.com/News/News.aspx/122460 (Accessed May 21, 2020).

[lii] "About the Temple Institute," Temple Institute, https://templeinstitute.org/about-us/ (accessed May 21, 2020).

[liii] Tom Clark, "What is the Abomination of Desolation? https://lifehopeandtruth.com/prophecy/understanding-the-book-of-daniel/abomination-of-desolation/ (Accessed May 22, 2020).

[liv] "Jeanne Nigro on the Jewish Temples," Lamb & Lion Ministries, https://christinprophecy.org/sermons/jeanne-nigro-on-the-jewish-temples/ (Accessed May 25, 2020).

[lv] Lambert Dolphin, "The Temple of Ezekiel," http://www.templemount.org/ezektmp.html, (Accessed May 25, 2020).

[lvi] Susan Pearlman, "What is Shalom: The True Meaning," http://www.templemount.org/ezektmp.html, (accessed May 26, 2020).

[lvii] Jack Wellman, "Guard Your Heart Bible Verse Meaning and Study,

https://www.patheos.com/blogs/christiancrier/2015/11/15/guard-your-heart-bible-verse-meaning-and-study/, (accessed May 26, 2020).

lviii Spiros Zodhiates, Th.D., *Hebrew-Greek Key Word Study Bible,* (Chattanooga: AMG Publishers, 1996), 2069.

lix Oz Torah, "Wandering Jew-Ask the Rabbi," https://www.oztorah.com/2010/07/wandering-jew-ask-the-rabbi/#.XvIeKJNKjaZ (accessed May 27, 2020).

Printed in Great Britain
by Amazon